LEISURE ARTS
PRESENTS

THE SPIRIT OF CHRISTMAS

CREATIVE
HOLIDAY IDEAS

BOOK FOURTEEN

Stockings hanging from the mantel, treasured ornaments tucked between evergreen boughs, and twinkling lights as far as the eye can see — these are just a few of the signs that the Christmas season is upon us. We celebrate the joyous occasion with those we hold dear, and offer splendidly wrapped gifts in honor of a very special birth. Transform your home into a holiday haven with ideas from this inspired volume. You'll find a festival of trims from elegant to rustic, creative handmade offerings, and delicious recipes for making your gatherings unforgettable. Here's wishing you and yours a Yuletide to remember, and may the spirit of Christmas linger the whole year through!

LEISURE ARTS, INC.
Little Rock, Arkansas

THE SPIRIT OF CHRISTMAS®
BOOK FOURTEEN

EDITORIAL STAFF

Vice President and Editor-in-Chief: Anne Van Wagner Childs
Executive Director: Sandra Graham Case
Design Director: Patricia Wallenfang Sowers
Test Kitchen Director/Foods Editor: Celia Fahr Harkey, R.D.
Editorial Director: Susan Frantz Wiles
Publications Director: Kristine Anderson Mertes
Creative Art Director: Gloria Bearden

PRODUCTION
DESIGN
Designers: Polly Tullis Browning, Diana Sanders Cates, Cherece Athy Cooper, Cyndi Hansen, Dani Martin, Sandra Spotts Ritchie, Billie Steward, Anne Pulliam Stocks, and Linda Diehl Tiano
Executive Assistant: Debra Smith

FOODS
Assistant Foods Editor: Jane Kenner Prather
Foods Copy Editor: Judy Millard
Test Kitchen Home Economists: Pat Coker and Rose Glass Klein
Test Kitchen Coordinator: Nora Faye Taylor

TECHNICAL
Managing Editor: Barbara Marguerite McClintock
Senior Technical Writer: Leslie Schick Gorrell
Technical Writers: Jennifer Potts Hutchings, Candice Treat Murphy, and Theresa Hicks Young
Technical Associates: Sherry Solida Ford, Linda Luder, and Kim Smith
Copy Editor: Susan Frazier
Production Assistant: Sharon Gillam

EDITORIAL
Managing Editor: Linda L. Trimble
Senior Associate Editor: Susan McManus Johnson
Associate Editors: Darla Burdette Kelsay, Stacey Robertson Marshall, and Suzie Puckett

ART
Book/Magazine Graphic Art Director: Diane Thomas
Graphic Artist: Mark R. Potter
Color Technician: Mark Hawkins
Staff Photographer: Russell Ganser
Photography Stylists: Sondra Daniel, Karen Smart Hall, Tiffany Huffman, Aurora Huston, Elizabeth Lackey, and Janna Laughlin
Publishing Systems Administrator: Becky Riddle
Publishing Systems Assistants: Myra Means and Chris Wertenberger

PROMOTIONS
Managing Editor: Alan Caudle
Associate Editor: Steven M. Cooper
Designer: Dale Rowett
Art Operations Director: Jeff Curtis
Graphic Artist: Deborah Kelly

"...and it was always said of him, that he knew how to keep Christmas well, if any man alive possessed the knowledge. May that be truly said of us, and all of us!"

— From *A Christmas Carol* by Charles Dickens

BUSINESS STAFF

Publisher: Rick Barton
Vice President, Finance: Tom Siebenmorgen
Vice President, Retail Marketing: Bob Humphrey
Director of Corporate Planning and Development: Laticia Mull Cornett
Vice President, National Accounts: Pam Stebbins

Retail Marketing Director: Margaret Sweetin
General Merchandise Manager: Cathy Laird
Vice President, Operations: Jim Dittrich
Distribution Director: Rob Thieme
Retail Customer Service Manager: Wanda Price
Print Production Manager: Fred F. Pruss

Library of Congress Catalog Card Number 98-65188
International Standard Book Number 1-57486-178-6

10 9 8 7 6 5 4 3 2 1

TABLE OF CONTENTS

TABLE OF CONTENTS
(Continued)

THE SHARING OF CHRISTMAS

Page 76

THE TASTES OF CHRISTMAS

Page 94

"TIMELESS" TRADITIONS......96

"SOUP-SATIONAL" OPEN HOUSE..........................100

SANTA'S BUNDLE OF SWEETS 108

BREAKFAST AT YOUR PACE......................114

THE SIGHTS OF CHRISTMAS

Nothing stirs the senses like the many exhilarating sights of Christmas. Whether you prefer the charming look of country crafts or the rich elegance of traditional trims, you'll love spicing up your decor with these spectacular Yuletide offerings. Indulge your creative side with our medley of unique ornaments for the evergreen, along with eye-catching table settings, wreaths, garlands, and decorations for every room of your home. Enjoy a memorable holiday with finery from our splendid collections!

"C" IS FOR CHRISTMAS

Capture the magic of an old-fashioned Christmas with winsome rag dolls and charming alphabet ornaments. Within these pages, you'll find a darling dimensional sampler to brighten your holiday mantel, as well as delightfully playful decorations for your tree. Best of all, the alphabet blocks lamp and lovable rag doll are treasures you can cherish year-round! Instructions for these projects and more, including the festive **Rag Doll Wreath** above, begin on page 12.

Travel back to the carefree days of childhood with this imaginative Christmas tree! **Doll Face Ornaments** (page 12), **Mini Samplers** (page 13), and **Wooden Alphabet Ornaments** (page 13) hang side by side with school bells, offering a bit of nostalgia for those Golden-Rule days. **"I Love Christmas" Hearts** (page 14) and **Homespun Heart Ornaments** (page 13) are super-simple designs that finish in a flash! Crafted from red felt and ordinary beverage cans, the **Painted Star Ornaments** (page 13) glow cheerily alongside faux candles and strands of bright wooden beads.

*C*leverly crafted from papier-mâché boxes, the **Alphabet Blocks Lamp** (page 12) will be fun and functional long after the holidays. The cute **Rag Doll** (page 13) is easier to make than you might think. She's a purchased doll form, just waiting for you to add her face, hair, and clothing!

Sweetly serene in her picture-perfect setting, the little dolly in our **Framed Sampler** (page 14) radiates good cheer. The simple verse recalls fond memories of a favorite childhood playmate.

"C" IS FOR CHRISTMAS

*School may be out for the holidays, but the fun is still in session with our clever "C" Is For Christmas Tree (shown on page 9). We gave it a gold star for its cheerful **Painted Star Ornaments** and purchased wooden bead garlands. Easy **Homespun Heart Ornaments** and "I Love Christmas" Hearts join shiny school bells for a warm touch of yesteryear. Perfect in plaid, the **Wooden Alphabet Ornaments** and **Mini Samplers** make "A+" additions to the tree. Even the full-size **Rag Doll** is sporting her ABC's on her buttoned and ruffled apron. She's a purchased cloth doll clad in an easy-to-make schoolgirl dress and striped stockings. In her "new" painted-on shoes, the precocious tomboy perches at the top of the tree while several **Doll Face Ornaments** peek out from the boughs below. With a few yards of cheery fabric wrapped 'round its base and purchased faux candles clipped to its branches, this evergreen finishes at the head of its class!*

DOLL FACE ORNAMENTS
(Shown on page 10)

For each ornament, you will need tracing paper; fabric marking pen; two 9" squares of muslin; polyester fiberfill; transfer paper; white, red, and black acrylic paint; paintbrushes; black permanent fine-point marker; drawing compass; 6" dia. lace-edged doily; two 4" x 8" pieces and one 2" x 12" piece of fabric; $1^{1}/_{2}$" x 16" strip of fabric; red cotton knit doll hair loops; hot glue gun; and 8" of clear nylon thread.

1. Trace head and face patterns, page 15, onto tracing paper; cut out. Use fabric marking pen to draw around head pattern on wrong side of one muslin square so that line is visible on right side. Use transfer paper to lightly transfer face to center of head on right side of muslin square.
2. Refer to *Tips For Painting On Fabric*, page 158, to paint face; allow to dry. Use marker to add details around eyes. Use both muslin squares and follow Steps 2 and 3 of *Sewing Shapes*, page 156, to make doll head. Stuff head with fiberfill. Sew opening closed.
3. Trace shoulders pattern, page 141, onto tracing paper; cut out. Using pattern and plaid rectangles, follow *Sewing Shapes* to sew shoulders, leaving a $1^{5}/_{8}$"w opening at center of straight edges.
4. Use compass to draw a $1^{5}/_{8}$" dia. circle at center of doily; cut out. Glue cut edge of doily along opening edge in shoulder.
5. For ruffle, matching wrong sides and long edges, press 2" x 12" fabric piece in half. Baste along long raw edges. Pull thread ends, gathering strip to fit around neck; glue ruffle around neck. Insert neck in shoulder opening and glue in place.
6. Arrange and glue doll hair on head. Tie $1^{1}/_{2}$" x 16" fabric strip into a bow; glue to head.
7. For hanger, use a needle to pull nylon thread through back of ornament. Knot thread ends together.

RAG DOLL WREATH
(Shown on page 8)

You will need yellow and red acrylic paint, paintbrushes, 4" x $5^{1}/_{2}$" chalkboard, $4^{1}/_{2}$"h bell with wooden handle, paper-backed fusible web, assorted fabrics, four $1^{1}/_{2}$" x $3^{1}/_{2}$" wooden hearts, decorative-edge craft scissors, hot glue gun, four $^{1}/_{2}$" dia. brown buttons, white paint pen, wooden star garland, one Doll Face Ornament (this page) without hanger, and an 18" dia. artificial evergreen wreath.

1. Paint frame of chalkboard yellow and handle of bell red; allow to dry.
2. Using a wooden heart as a pattern, follow *Making Appliqués*, page 156, to make four heart appliqués from fabrics. Using craft scissors to cut out appliqués, make two $^{3}/_{8}$" x $3^{5}/_{8}$" and two $^{3}/_{8}$" x 5" border appliqués from fabrics for chalkboard.
3. Fuse fabric hearts to wooden hearts. Fuse borders on chalkboard frame. Glue one button to each corner of frame. Use paint pen to write on chalkboard: "C" is for Christmas.
4. Tear three $1^{3}/_{4}$" x 14" fabric strips. Tie each fabric strip into a bow.

Arrange and glue garland, ornament, chalkboard, bell, hearts, and bows on wreath.

ALPHABET BLOCKS LAMP
(Shown on page 11)

You will need a hot glue gun; one $^{3}/_{4}$" x $8^{1}/_{2}$" x $8^{1}/_{2}$" wooden square and one $^{3}/_{4}$" x $10^{1}/_{2}$" x $10^{1}/_{2}$" wooden square; craft drill; gold, red, blue, and green acrylic paint; paintbrushes; glossy wood-tone spray; four assorted wooden beads with $^{3}/_{8}$" dia. holes; four 1" dia. wooden beads for feet; $3^{1}/_{4}$"w puffed wooden heart; paper-backed fusible web; assorted fabrics for lamp base appliqués; one each $2^{3}/_{4}$", $4^{1}/_{2}$", and $5^{1}/_{2}$" square papier-mâché boxes without lids; craft knife; lamp wiring kit; three $3^{3}/_{4}$"h wooden letters; assorted buttons; self-adhesive lampshade kit; and fabric to cover lampshade.

Allow paint and wood-tone spray to dry after each application.

1. For lamp base, center and glue $8^{1}/_{2}$" square on $10^{1}/_{2}$" wooden square. Drill a $^{1}/_{2}$" dia. hole in center of base.
2. Follow *Painting Techniques*, page 157, to paint lamp base green, beads for feet and heart red, and remaining beads red and blue. Apply wood-tone spray to painted items. Glue feet to corners of bottom of base.
3. For borders around each box, fuse web to wrong sides of desired fabrics. Cut one fabric square to fit bottom of box. Cut sixteen $^{1}/_{2}$"w fabric strips the length of each side. Fuse square to

bottom of box. Overlapping ends as necessary, fuse one strip along each side edge of box. Use craft knife to cut a $^1/_2$" dia. hole in center bottom of box.

4. Aligning holes, stack boxes bottom side up on lamp base. Follow manufacturer's instructions to assemble lamp, adding three assorted beads to pipe stem before threading stem through boxes and base.

5. For each wooden letter, draw around letter in reverse on web side of fabric; cut out just inside drawn line. Fuse fabric letter to front of wooden letter.

6. Glue letters, heart, and buttons to lamp.

7. Follow manufacturer's instructions to cover lampshade with fabric. For finial, glue remaining bead at center top of lampshade.

PAINTED STAR ORNAMENTS
(Shown on page 10)

For each ornament, you will need utility scissors, aluminum beverage can, tracing paper, black permanent fine-point marker, white spray primer, yellow and red spray paint, glossy wood-tone spray, red dimensional paint, foam brush, matte varnish, wood glue, red felt, pinking shears, button, push pin, red embroidery floss, $^1/_8$" dia. hole punch, and 8" of red baby rickrack.

Allow primer, paint, wood-tone spray, varnish, and glue to dry after each application.

1. Use utility scissors to cut through opening and down to bottom of beverage can; cut away top and bottom of can. Flatten can piece.

2. Trace star and heart A patterns, page 15, onto tracing paper; cut out.

3. Use marker to draw around heart and star pattern on beverage can piece; cut out. Apply primer to one side of each shape. Paint star yellow and heart red. Apply wood-tone spray to star. Use dimensional paint to paint dots along edges of star. Use foam brush to apply varnish to heart and star.

4. Glue star to felt. Leaving a $^3/_8$" border, use pinking shears to cut star from felt. Center heart on star, then button on heart. Using holes in button as a guide, use push pin to make two holes through heart and star. Use floss to sew button to ornament, tying ends at front.

5. For hanger, use hole punch to punch hole through one point of star. Thread rickrack through hole; knot ends together.

WOODEN ALPHABET ORNAMENTS
(Shown on page 10)

For each ornament, you will need yellow acrylic paint, paintbrush, $3^3/_4$"h wooden letter, paper-backed fusible web, fabric scrap, tan card stock, hot glue gun, black permanent medium-point marker, and 12" of floral wire.

1. Paint letter yellow; allow to dry. Fuse web to wrong side of fabric; do not remove paper backing. Draw around letter in reverse on web side of fabric; cut out just inside drawn line. Fuse fabric letter to front of wooden letter.

2. Draw around outside only of letter on card stock; cut out $^3/_8$" outside drawn line. Glue letter on card stock shape.

3. Use marker to draw "stitches" around letter on card stock. For hanger, bend each end of wire into a "U" shape. Glue one end to back of ornament.

MINI SAMPLERS
(Shown on page 10)

For each sampler, you will need fabric for borders, craft glue, $4^3/_4$" x 6" piece of tan card stock, buttons, paper-backed fusible web, black permanent fine-point marker, and 6"w mini clothes hanger.

Allow glue to dry after each application.

1. Tear two $^3/_4$" x $4^3/_4$" strips and two $^3/_4$" x $5^1/_2$" strips from fabric. Glue fabric strips along edges of card stock.

2. Using "A," "B," or "C" patterns, page 142, follow *Making Appliqués*, page 156, to make desired letter appliqué. Arrange appliqué on card stock; fuse in place.

3. Using marker and dashed lines, write "is for A sweet Noel" for A sampler, "is for be good" for B sampler, or "is for Christmas" for C sampler on card stock. Glue buttons to corners.

4. For hanging tabs, tear two $^1/_2$" x 2" strips from fabric. Matching short ends, fold strips in half over hanger; glue ends together. Glue tabs to back of card stock along top edge.

HOMESPUN HEART ORNAMENTS
(Shown on page 10)

For each ornament, you will need a papier-mâché ball ornament (we used $2^1/_2$", 3", and 4" dia. ornaments), red acrylic paint, paintbrush, and a black permanent fine-point marker.

Paint a red heart on ornament; allow to dry. Use marker to draw "stitches" around heart.

RAG DOLL
(Shown on page 11)

You will need tracing paper; transfer paper; 22"h muslin doll body; white, red, and black acrylic paint; paintbrushes; black permanent fine-point marker; polyurethane semi-gloss varnish; red cotton knit doll hair loops; $1^1/_2$" x 16" torn fabric strip; $^1/_4$ yd. of red-and-white striped 45"w fabric; hot glue gun; straight pins; plaid fabric for dress; snaps; unbleached muslin for apron; paper-backed fusible web; fabric scraps for appliqués; and buttons.

Allow paint and varnish to dry after each application. Match right sides and raw edges and use a $^1/_4$" seam allowance for all sewing unless otherwise indicated.

1. Trace face pattern, page 15, onto tracing paper. Use transfer paper to transfer face to front of doll's head. Paint face on doll. Use marker to add details to eyes.

2. For shoes, paint doll's feet black. Apply varnish to shoes.

3. Arrange hair loops on head and stitch in place. Tie torn fabric strip into a bow; tack to head.

4. For each stocking, cut an 8" square from striped fabric. Press each edge 1/4" to wrong side. Matching one edge with top of shoe and overlapping edges at back, wrap square around leg. Glue edge of stocking to leg along top of shoe. Catching leg in stitching, hand sew stocking seam at back.

5. Refer to bodice diagram, page 15, and use tracing paper to make bodice pattern. Cut a 10" × 21" piece of plaid fabric. Matching long edges, fold fabric in half from top to bottom. Fold again from right to left. Use pattern to cut out bodice. For back opening, unfold and cut bodice down center back. Press each raw edge of back opening 1/4" to wrong side twice; stitch in place.

6. For neck ruffle, cut a 2" × 24" strip from plaid fabric. Press short ends 1/4" to wrong side. Matching wrong sides and long edges, baste 1/4" from raw edges. Gather ruffle to fit bodice neck opening; pin in place. Sew ruffle to bodice. Press seam allowance toward bodice; topstitch in place.

7. Press raw edge of sleeve 1/4" to wrong side twice; sew in place. Sew underarm and side seams of bodice.

8. For skirt, cut a 10" × 45" piece of fabric. For hem, press one long edge 1/4" then 1/2" to wrong side; sew in place. For skirt back opening, press each short edge 1/4" to wrong side twice; sew in place. Baste 1/4" from remaining raw edge. Pull basting threads, gathering skirt to fit bottom edge of bodice; pin in place. Sew skirt to bodice. Sew snaps along back of dress opening. Place dress on doll.

9. For apron, cut a 17" × 20" piece of muslin. Press short edges 1/4" to wrong side. Matching right sides and long edges, fold apron in half. Sew long edges together (top). Turn right side out; press. Topstitch along side edges.

10. For apron ties, cut a 2 1/2" × 42" strip from muslin. Press each edge 1/4" to wrong side. Matching wrong sides, fold strip in half lengthwise. Topstitch along pressed edges.

11. Baste 1 1/2" from top of apron. Pull basting threads, drawing up gathers to measure 7 1/2". Centering ties over gathers on right side of apron, stitch ties to apron.

12. For each shoulder strap, cut a 2 1/2" × 6" strip from muslin. Refer to Step 10 to make each shoulder strap.

13. Place apron on doll. Use pins to mark placement for shoulder straps on apron and ties. Remove apron. Sew straps to wrong sides of apron and ties.

14. Using patterns, page 142, follow *Making Appliqués*, page 156, to make one each of "A," "B," and "C" appliqués from fabric scraps. Arrange appliqués on apron; fuse in place. Sew buttons to apron. Replace apron on doll.

FRAMED SAMPLER
(Shown on page 11)

You will need a 16" × 19" wooden frame with a 10 1/2" × 14" opening and a flat inner edge at least 2" wide; white, red, green, and black acrylic paint; paintbrushes; poster board; paper-backed fusible web; muslin; black permanent medium-point marker; ruler; fabric for frame border; tracing paper; transfer paper; scraps of assorted fabrics for appliqués; drawing compass; 6" dia. doily; fabric glue; 12" of 1/4"w green satin ribbon; assorted buttons; red cotton knit doll hair loops; and a 1 1/2" × 16" torn fabric strip.

Allow paint to dry after each application.

1. Paint frame green. For background, cut a piece of poster board, fusible web, and muslin to fit frame opening. Fuse muslin to poster board.

2. Mount muslin-covered poster board in frame. Use marker and ruler to draw a dashed line 1/4" from each inside edge. Remove poster board from frame.

3. Cut 2"w fabric strips to fit around frame opening. Mitering corners, glue in place.

4. Trace verse pattern, page 142, and face pattern, page 15, onto tracing paper. Leaving room for appliqués and bodice, use transfer paper to transfer patterns to muslin-covered poster board.

5. Paint face. Use marker to add details to eyes.

6. Using patterns, pages 15, 141, and 142, follow *Making Appliqués*, page 156, to make one each bodice, "A," "B," and "C" appliqués, and four heart B appliqués from fabric scraps.

7. Use compass to draw a 1 5/8" dia. circle in center of doily; cut out. For collar, cut doily in half; discard one half. Press straight edge 1/4" to wrong side. Insert straight edge of bodice appliqué into fold of collar.

8. Arrange appliqués on frame and background; fuse in place. Spot glue straight edge of collar to secure. Use marker to draw over transferred words and to draw "stitches" around "A," "B," and "C" appliqués.

9. Tie ribbon into a bow. Glue bow and button to neck. Arrange and glue hair loops around face. Tie fabric strip into a bow. Glue bow to hair. Glue one button to center of each heart on frame. Arrange and glue buttons on background.

10. Mount design in frame.

"I LOVE CHRISTMAS" HEARTS
(Shown on page 10)

For each ornament, you will need 6"w wooden heart with hanger; white, red, and brown acrylic paint; paintbrushes; soft cloth; and 20" of 1/4"w white satin ribbon.

1. Paint heart red; allow to dry. Use white paint to paint "I ♥ Christmas" on heart; allow to dry.

2. To give ornament an aged look, thin brown paint with one part water to one part paint. Brush thinned paint over ornament. While paint is still wet, wipe with soft cloth; allow to dry.

3. Replace hanger with ribbon.

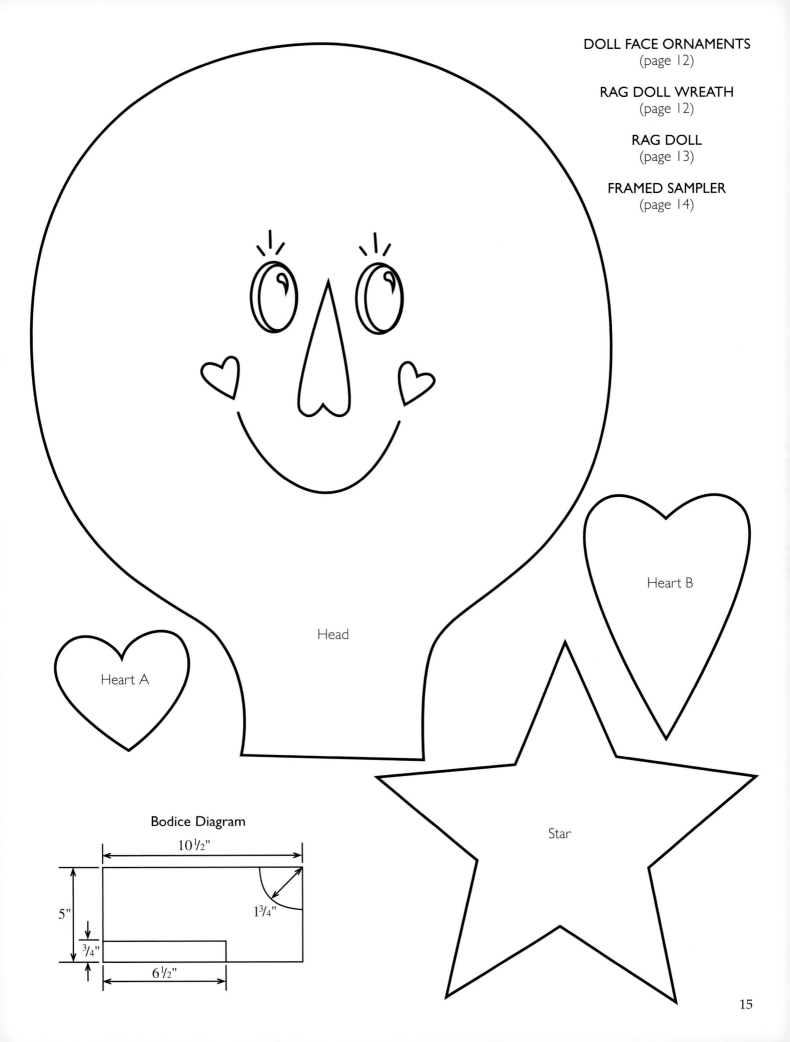

Heart B

Head

Heart A

Star

Bodice Diagram

10½"

5"

¾"

1¾"

6½"

Journey to Bethlehem

Join the Magi in their search for the Christ Child with our beautiful appliquéd **Advent Wall Hanging.** With the largest star representing December 1, begin on December 2 to button one golden star per day to the royal-blue sky. When each button holds a star, it's Christmas Day! Pair the calendar with the matching **Wise Men Pillow** for a gentle reminder that, above all, wise men still seek Him! Instructions begin on page 18.

WISE MEN PILLOW
(Shown on page 17)

 You will need tailor's chalk, two 19½" squares of blue fabric for pillow front and back, sewing thread, paper-backed fusible web, fabric scraps for appliqués, clear nylon thread, stabilizer, fabric glue, 1 yd. of ⅛"w gold trim, ½"w gold star shank button, 1¾ yds. of ¼"w gold trim, and polyester fiberfill.

1. Use chalk to mark a line 2½" from each edge on right side of pillow front for appliqué placement.
2. Use patterns, pages 19, 152, and 153, and follow *Making Appliqués*, page 156, to make large star and wise men appliqués from fabrics. Arrange appliqués on pillow front; fuse in place. Use nylon thread and follow *Machine Appliqué*, page 156, to stitch over raw edges of appliqués.
3. Glue lengths of ⅛"w trim to star and pillow front for star rays and to wise men for trim on clothing; allow to dry. Sew button to center of star appliqué.
4. Place pillow front and back right sides together. Leaving a 2" long opening for turning, stitch ½" from raw edges. Clip corners; turn right side out.
5. Leaving a 2" long opening on same side as opening for turning and trim unstitched at opening, sew ¼"w trim over chalk line, mitering corners as necessary (Fig. 1). Stuff pillow with fiberfill. Sew both openings closed, stitching remaining trim in place.

Fig. 1

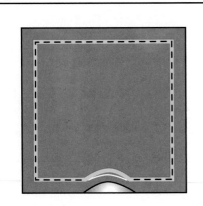

ADVENT WALL HANGING
(Shown on page 16)

 You will need gold spray paint, 22" of ½" dia. wooden dowel, two 3"w papier-mâché stars, 24 small (⅜" to ½" dia.) buttons, ⅝ yd. blue fabric, fusible interfacing, clear nylon thread, sewing thread, 2 yds. of ½"w gold braid trim, ¾"w paper-backed fusible web tape, paper-backed fusible web, scraps of assorted fabrics for appliqués, stabilizer, tracing paper, transfer paper, gold dimensional paint, gold metallic thread, one ¾" dia. gold metallic shank button, gold fabric for Advent stars, craft knife, cutting mat, hot glue gun, and 1 yd. of ¼" dia. gold cord.

1. Spray paint dowel, stars, and small buttons gold; allow to dry.
2. For background, cut one 19½" × 27" piece each from blue fabric and fusible interfacing. Fuse interfacing to wrong side of fabric.
3. For casing, fuse web tape along one short edge on wrong side of background; do not remove paper backing. Press edge 2" to wrong side; remove paper backing and fuse in place.
4. Use patterns, pages 19, 152, and 153, and follow *Making Appliqués*, page 156, to make one each of large star, wise men, and tree trunk appliqués and two (one in reverse) of each palm frond appliqués from fabrics.
5. Arrange appliqués on background; fuse in place. Use nylon thread and follow *Machine Appliqué*, page 156, to stitch over raw edges of appliqués.
6. Trace "They Followed the Star" pattern, page 19, onto tracing paper; use transfer paper to transfer onto background. Use dimensional paint to paint over words; allow to dry. Use gold thread to sew ¾" dia. button to large star and small buttons randomly to background.
7. For Advent stars, fuse interfacing to wrong side of gold fabric. Trace small star pattern, this page, onto tracing paper; cut out. Draw around pattern 24 times on wrong side of fused fabric; cut out stars. Use craft knife and cutting mat to cut a ½" long slit for button in center of each star.
8. Mitering corners, glue trim along bottom and side edges of wall hanging.
9. Referring to Fig. 1, use craft knife to cut a ½" dia. hole in back of each papier-mâché star. Insert dowel through casing at top of banner. Glue one star onto each end of dowel. For hanger, knot ends of cord at each end of dowel.

Fig. 1

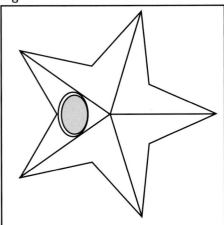

Small Star

They Followed the Star

Large
Star

Tartan Classics

Bring a delightful mix of the Scottish Highlands and the English moors "across the pond" to America and into your holiday celebrations! We've gathered a fabulous collection of accents to brighten your home with colorful plaids, ruffled medallions, and regal red ribbons. To recreate these festive designs, including the **Ruffled Tartan Trees** shown here atop brass candlesticks, turn to page 26.

A clock ornament and rose appliqué are perfect accents for our vibrant **Shirred Pillow** (page 28) and **Envelope Pillow** (page 27). Here's a splendid finishing touch for your tartan-inspired tree! A rich **Ruffled Tree Skirt** (page 26) is bountifully edged with gathered fabric and elegant braid.

Beribboned
*Medallion
Ornaments*
(page 26) add
regal touches
to the boughs
of this *Tartan
Classics Tree*
(page 26),
while *Holly Bow
Ornaments*
(page 26) and
*Gathered Fabric
Ornaments*
(page 26) are
superbly simple
to create. Doing
double duty as
either gift boxes or
ornaments, papier-
mâché *Scottie
Boxes* (page 27)
are topped with
appliqués of spunky
terriers in jaunty
little jackets.
*Stitched Clock
Ornaments*
(page 27) count
down the minutes
to midnight,
reminding us of the
Scottish tradition
of celebrating
the new year
in a big way!

When these cheery **Medallion Stockings** (page 30) grace the mantel, the Yuletide can't help but be very merry indeed! Shiny stocking hangers and rows of gleaming candlesticks echo the tiny touches of gold cord running 'round the medallion buttons. Holly and ivy, both a part of British Christmas tradition, look right at home with the evergreen garland. In fact, the berry-laden greenery makes an eye-catching stocking filler — at least until Father Christmas replaces the sprigs with special gifts!

This **Scottie Chairback Cover** (*page 29*) will make your dinner guests feel like royalty! Set a memorable table this Christmas with our **Tartan Place Mat and Napkin** (*pages 28, 29*), **"Cracker" Party Favor** (*page 29*), and **Decoupaged Plate** (*page 27*). They're perfectly accented by a shining brass charger and a **Small Topiary Placecard** (*page 30*).

Tartan Classics

Cheerily festooned with items to charm any Anglophile, this **Tartan Classics Tree** (shown on page 21) has holly and ivy added for extra fullness. Purchased brass horns and miniature teacups are oh-so-English accents that shine beside the little electric candles. The boughs are generously laden with gold cord, shimmering tassels, and bright beaded garland. Large jingle bells tied with festive bows add a merry note. Of course, for a wee bit of the Highlands there must be tartan plaid, and the perky terriers on the **Scottie Boxes** are wearing their colors with pride! The **Medallion Ornaments**, **Holly Bow Ornaments**, and **Gathered Fabric Ornaments** all finish in a twinkle, while **Stitched Clock Ornaments** with fob chains attached are easy designs adding their own timely touch. The **Houndstooth Bow** at top and the **Ruffled Tree Skirt** at bottom make a grand finale to this very British tree!

MEDALLION ORNAMENTS

(Shown on page 23)

For each ornament, you will need a 1" dia. self-covered button, fabric to cover button, hot glue gun, 5" of narrow gold cord, 4" x 14" fabric strip, sewing thread, 18" of 1 1/2"w double-sided satin ribbon, and 8" of floral wire.

1. Follow manufacturer's instructions to cover button with fabric. Overlapping ends as necessary, glue cord around button.
2. Press one short edge of fabric strip to wrong side. Matching wrong sides and long edges, fold fabric strip in half. Leaving a 4" tail at each end, baste along long edges. Pull thread ends to gather strip into a circle; knot and trim ends. Insert short raw end inside pressed end; tack to secure. Glue button to center of circle.
3. Crisscrossing ends, fold ribbon in half to form a loop; spot glue to secure. Glue circle to loop. For hanger, bend each end of wire into a "U" shape; glue one end to back of ornament.

HOUNDSTOOTH BOW

(Shown on page 21)

You will need a 2" dia. self-covered button, fabric to cover button, hot glue gun, 7" of 1/8"w gold cord, 4" x 20" fabric strip, 3 1/2 yds. of 2 1/2"w wired ribbon, and 8" of floral wire.

1. Follow Steps 1 and 2 of Medallion Ornament, this page, to make medallion for bow.

2. Referring to *Making a Bow*, page 157, make a bow with four 12" loops and two 36" streamers. Glue medallion to center of bow. Use wire ends to wire bow to tree topper.

RUFFLED TREE SKIRT

(Shown on page 22)

You will need a 45" square of red fabric for skirt, fabric marking pencil, thumbtack, string, 2 1/2 yds. of red plaid fabric for ruffle, straight pins, and 4 yds. of 1"w gold trim.

1. Using a 2" measurement for inside cutting line and a 22" measurement for outside cutting line, follow Steps 2 - 4 of *Cutting a Fabric Circle*, page 156, to cut tree skirt from skirt fabric; unfold.
2. For back opening, cut from center to outer edge of skirt.
3. Press inner circle and straight opening edges 1/4" to wrong side twice; topstitch along pressed edges.
4. Cut an 11"w strip 10 yds. long (pieced as necessary) from ruffle fabric. Matching right sides and long edges, fold ruffle in half. Sew across short ends. Turn right side out; press. Leaving a 4" tail at each end, baste along long raw edges. Pulling thread ends, gather ruffle to fit outer edge of skirt; knot and trim ends. Matching raw edges, pin ruffle to right side of skirt. Use a 1/2" seam allowance to sew ruffle to skirt. Press seam allowance toward skirt.
5. Folding 1/2" of trim ends to wrong side of skirt, sew trim to skirt along ruffle seam.

GATHERED FABRIC ORNAMENTS

(Shown on page 23)

For each ornament, you will need a 14" square of fabric, fabric marking pen, thumbtack, string, 3" dia. plastic foam ball, rubber band, 10" of 3/8" dia. cord, hot glue gun, 14" of 1 1/2"w wired ribbon, 1" dia. self-covered button, and fabric to cover button.

1. Using a 7" measurement for cutting line, follow Steps 2 - 4 of *Cutting a Fabric Circle*, page 156, to cut a circle from 14" fabric square.
2. Place ball at center on wrong side of fabric circle. Gather circle around ball; secure gathers with rubber band.
3. For hanger, fold cord in half; glue ends of cord to wrong side of fabric under rubber band. Tie ribbon into a bow around gathers, covering rubber band.
4. Follow manufacturer's instructions to cover button with fabric. Glue button to center of bow.

HOLLY BOW ORNAMENTS

(Shown on page 23)

For each ornament, you will need a 10" x 25" fabric strip, 8" of floral wire, hot glue gun, artificial holly stem, and three 7/8" dia. gold jingle bells.

1. Press long edges of fabric 2 1/2" to wrong side. Overlap ends 2" to form circle. With overlap at center back gather fabric at center to form bow. Secure gathers with wire.
2. Glue holly and bells to front of bow. Use wire ends to wire bow to tree.

SCOTTIE BOXES
(Shown on page 23)

For each box, you will need a 1 1/2" x 3 1/4" x 4 1/4" oval papier-mâché box with lid; red, black-and-white check, and coordinating plaid fabrics to cover box; spray adhesive; tracing paper; paper-backed fusible web; plaid and black fabrics for appliqués; hot glue gun; and 8" of 1/2"w gold mesh ribbon.

1. Remove lid from box. For side of box, cut a 2 1/2" x 13" strip from plaid fabric. Press one short edge of strip 1/2" to wrong side. For bottom of box, draw around box on wrong side of plaid fabric. Cut out oval 1/8" inside drawn line.
2. Apply spray adhesive to wrong side of cut fabric pieces. Beginning with raw short edge and aligning one long edge with top of box, smooth fabric onto side of box and over bottom edge, clipping as necessary. Smooth oval onto bottom of box.
3. For top of lid, draw around lid on wrong side of red fabric; cut out oval 1/4" outside drawn line. Use patterns, page 30, and follow *Making Appliqués*, page 156, to make one dog appliqué from black fabric and one sweater appliqué from plaid fabric. Overlapping as necessary, fuse shapes to oval. Apply spray adhesive to wrong side of oval; smooth onto top of lid and over onto sides, clipping as necessary.
4. For side of lid, cut a strip of fabric 1" x 13". Press one short end of strip 1/2" to wrong side. Press long edges of strip 1/4" to wrong side. Beginning with raw end, glue strip around lid.
5. Tie ribbon into a bow. Glue bow to dog.

STITCHED CLOCK ORNAMENTS
(Shown on page 23)

For each ornament, you will need black embroidery floss, 6" square of 22 ct. white Hardanger fabric, antique gold and black spray paint, 3 1/4" dia. gold decorative frame, and 9" of gold chain with clasp for hanger.

Refer to French Knot, page 158, and Backstitch, page 159, before beginning project. Use 2 strands of floss for all stitching.

1. Center and work clock face design, page 30, over two fabric threads on Hardanger.
2. Remove backing and mounting pieces from frame. Apply antique gold paint to frame; allow to dry. Lightly apply black paint over gold; allow to dry.
3. Center backing over design area of stitched piece. Use a pencil to lightly draw around backing. Cut out stitched design along drawn line. Mount design and backing in frame. Attach chain to hanger of frame.

DECOUPAGED PLATE
(Shown on page 25)

You will need a grease pencil, clear glass plate (we used a 9 7/8" dia. plate), liquid gold leaf, paintbrushes, paper towel, drawing compass, liquid fray preventative, floral motif fabric and black-and-white checked fabric for decoupage, liquid laminate, soft cloth, sponge, and PermEnamel™ surface conditioner, white paint, and sealer.

Allow gold leaf, surface conditioner, fray preventative, and sealer to dry after each application unless otherwise indicated.

1. Use grease pencil to draw scalloped border on top of plate along outer edge. Use gold leaf to paint border on back of plate. Use paper towel to remove pencil. Apply surface conditioner to back of plate.
2. Measure diameter of area on back of plate to be covered with fabric. Use compass to draw a circle the determined measurement on wrong side of checked fabric; cut out. Cut desired motif from floral fabric. Apply fray preventative to edges of circle and motif.

3. Wet floral motif with water. Apply liquid laminate over area on back of plate to be covered with fabric. While laminate is wet, center right side of motif on back of plate. Use fingers to press out air bubbles. Use cloth to wipe away excess laminate; allow to dry.
4. Using circle, repeat Step 3 to apply right side of fabric to back of plate. Allow to dry 24 hours. Sponge conditioner over area on back of plate not covered by fabric. Being careful not to get paint on fabric, paint conditioned area of plate white; allow to dry two hours. Repeat application of conditioner and paint. Apply two to three coats of sealer to back of plate.

ENVELOPE PILLOW
(Shown on page 22)

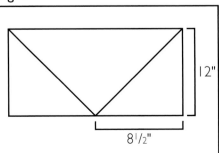

You will need two 12" x 17" pieces of black-and-white checked fabric for flap, floral motif fabric for appliqué, paper-backed fusible web, clear thread, 1 yd. of red and gold braid, 18" x 19" piece of red plaid fabric for wide band, 2 1/2" x 19" piece of blue plaid fabric for narrow band, 3/4"w paper-backed fusible web tape, 19" square each of red and red plaid fabrics for pillow front and back, 2 1/4 yds. of gold cord with lip, and polyester fiberfill.

Match right sides and raw edges and use a 1/2" seam allowance for all sewing unless otherwise indicated.

1. Matching right sides and edges, place flap pieces together. Refer to Fig. 1 to draw cutting lines. Cut out flap pieces.

Fig. 1

12"

8 1/2"

2. Fuse web to wrong side of desired motif on floral fabric; cut out. Remove paper backing. With center point of flap piece at bottom, center motif on right side of one flap piece. Using clear thread, follow *Machine Appliqué,* page 156, to sew over edges of appliqué.

3. Leaving long edge open, sew flap pieces together. Clip corner and turn right side out; press. Sew opening closed. Sew red and gold braid along short edges of flap.

4. Matching wrong sides and short edges, fold wide band in half; press. Press long raw edges of narrow band $3/4$" to wrong side. Fuse web tape to wrong side of narrow band. Fuse narrow band along pressed edge of wide band. Place wrong side of wide band on right side of pillow front. Place wrong side of flap on right side of band. Aligning raw edges, baste flap and band to pillow front.

5. Matching raw edges and overlapping ends, baste cord around edges of pillow front. Matching right sides, using a zipper foot, and leaving an opening for turning, sew pillow front and back together. Clip corners; turn right side out. Stuff pillow with fiberfill; sew opening closed.

SHIRRED PILLOW
(Shown on page 28)

You will need heavy-duty thread, 33" square of red fabric, two 23" squares of plaid fabric for pillow front and back, $2^1/2$ yds. of $1/2$" dia. gold cord with lip, polyester fiberfill, two $1^1/2$" dia. red buttons, long needle, household cement, and one Stitched Clock Ornament (page 27) without chain.

Use a $1/2$" seam allowance for all sewing unless otherwise indicated.

1. Press two opposite edges of 33" square $1/2$" to wrong side. For shirring, baste along both remaining edges. Pull thread ends to gather edges to 23".

2. Matching wrong side of shirring to right side of pillow front, baste shirred edges to edges of pillow front. Matching raw edges on right side of

pillow front and overlapping cord ends, baste cord to pillow front.

3. Matching right sides, using a zipper foot, and leaving an opening for turning, sew pillow front and back together. Clip corners; turn right side out. Stuff with fiberfill; sew opening closed.

4. Gather shirring at center of pillow. Secure with thread. Place button on center back of pillow. Place remaining button at center of shirring. Working through button on back of pillow, use long needle and heavy-duty thread to sew button to center of pillow front.

5. Cement ornament to button on pillow front; allow to dry.

RUFFLED TARTAN TREES
(Shown on page 20)

You will need 12"h and 16"h plastic foam cones, plaid fabrics, straight pins, hot glue gun, batting, and two Medallion Ornaments (page 26) without hangers.

1. For each cone, cut two 6" squares of fabric. Pleating as necessary and using pins to secure fabric to cone, cover top of cone with one square and bottom of cone with remaining square.

2. For large tree, cut the following strips from fabrics: 9" x 21", 10" x 32", 12" x 42", 13" x 45", and 15" x 46".

3. For small tree, cut the following strips from fabrics: 8" x 21", 10" x 33", 10" x 38", and 12" x 42".

4. For each tree, matching wrong sides and long edges, fold fabric strips in half; press. Leaving a 4" tail at each end, baste along long raw edges. Beginning with largest strip near base of cone, pull thread ends to gather strips around cone, ending with smallest strip at point of cone. Glue gathered edges to cone.

5. To add fullness, measure around cones under each fabric layer. Cut pieces of batting 6" by the determined measurement. Beginning at one long edge on each piece, roll batting pieces. Glue batting rolls around cone under fabric layers.

6. Glue one ornament to top of each tree.

TARTAN PLACE MAT
(Shown on page 25)

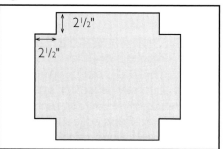

You will need $12^1/2$" x 17" piece of fabric for top layer, 15" x 20" piece of fabric for middle layer, and a $15^3/4$" x 21" piece of fabric for bottom layer; paper-backed fusible web; $1/2$"w paper-backed fusible web tape; straight pins; clear nylon thread; $1^1/3$ yds. of gold braid trim; four $1^1/2$" dia. self-covered buttons; fabric to cover buttons; hot glue gun; and wire cutters.

1. Fuse web to wrong side of top layer fabric piece. Do not remove paper backing.

2. Cut a $2^1/2$" square from each corner of middle layer fabric piece (Fig. 1).

Fig. 1

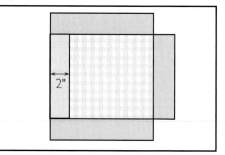

3. For place mat, remove paper backing from top layer. Center and fuse top layer to wrong side of middle layer.

4. Press one short edge of middle layer $1/2$" to wrong side. Fuse web tape along pressed edge on wrong side of middle layer. Do not remove paper backing. Press edge 2" to wrong side (Fig. 2). Unfold edge and remove paper backing. Refold edge and fuse in place. Repeat for remaining short edge of middle layer.

Fig. 2

5. Press one corner of one long edge of middle layer diagonally to wrong side as shown in Fig. 3; fuse web tape along diagonal edge (Fig. 4). Do not remove paper backing. Repeat for remaining three corners.

Fig. 3

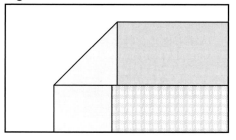

Fig. 4

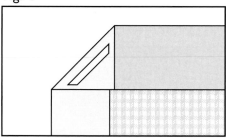

6. Press one long raw edge of middle layer ¹/₂" to wrong side. Fuse web tape along pressed edges on wrong side of fabric piece. Do not remove paper backing. Press edge 2" to wrong side. Unfold edge and remove paper backing from long and diagonal edges. Refold edge and fuse in place. Repeat for remaining raw edge of middle layer.

7. Using 1³/₄" in place of 2¹/₂", refer to Fig. 1 to cut a 1³/₄" square from each corner of bottom layer fabric piece. Center place mat on wrong side of bottom layer; pin in place. Using 1¹/₄" measurement in place of 2" measurement to cover edge of place mat, follow Steps 4 - 6 to make outer border. Use clear thread to sew along inner edge of bottom layer. Remove pins. Glue trim along inner edge of place mat.

8. Follow manufacturer's instructions to cover buttons with fabric. Use wire cutters to cut shanks from buttons. Glue buttons to corners of place mat over trim.

TARTAN NAPKIN
(Shown on page 25)

You will need two 18" squares of fabric and 30" of 1¹/₂"w ribbon.

1. Matching right sides and leaving an opening for turning, use ¹/₄" seam allowance to sew fabric pieces together. Clip corners and turn right side out; press. Topstitch along edges.

2. Gather napkin; tie ribbon into a bow around gathers.

"CRACKER" PARTY FAVOR
(Shown on page 25)

For each favor, you will need one 2" x 8" small fabric piece and one 8" x 10" large fabric piece, 2" x 8" piece of paper-backed fusible web, ¹/₂"w fusible web tape, fabric glue, two 8" and two 10" pieces of ¹/₄"w gold braid, 2" dia. tube from a roll of gift wrap, and a favor to fit in cracker.

1. Fuse web to wrong side of small fabric piece. For wrapper, matching short edges of small fabric piece to long edges of large fabric piece, center and fuse small fabric piece to right side of large fabric piece. Glue one 8" length of braid over each long edge of small fabric piece.

2. Fuse web tape along wrong side of short edges of wrapper. Do not remove paper backing. Press short edges ¹/₂" to wrong side. Unfold edge and remove paper backing. Refold edge and fuse in place. Repeat, fusing web tape to one long edge of wrapper.

3. Cut a 5" length from tube. Roll 5" tube piece in center of wrapper. Gather wrapper at one end of tube. Tie a 10" length of braid into a bow around gathers. Place favor in tube. Gather and secure remaining end of wrapper with a second 10" length of braid.

SCOTTIE CHAIRBACK COVER
(Shown on page 25)

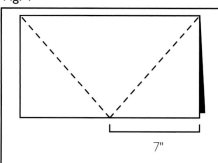

You will need a 14¹/₂" x 26" piece of blue plaid fabric for bottom layer, 13" x 24¹/₂" piece of fabric for middle layer, 11" x 22¹/₂" piece of red solid fabric for top layer, fabric marking pen, matching thread, straight pins, gold braid, plaid and black fabrics for appliqués, tracing paper, paper-backed fusible web, 8" of ¹/₄"w gold mesh ribbon, hot glue gun, and a Medallion Ornament (page 26).

1. Matching long edges, fold blue plaid fabric piece in half. Refer to Fig. 1 to cut a point at each short end.

Fig. 1

7"

2. Using a 6¹/₄" measurement for red plaid fabric piece and a 5¹/₄" measurement for red solid fabric piece refer to Step 1 to cut a point at short ends of each fabric piece.

3. Press all edges of each layer ¹/₄" to wrong side twice. Topstitch close to outer edges on bottom layer only. Center middle and top layers on bottom layer. Topstitch ¹/₈" from edges of middle and top layers.

4. Glue trim to chairback cover ¹/₄" inside edges of top layer.

5. Use patterns, page 30, and follow *Making Appliqués*, page 156, to make one dog appliqué from black fabric and one sweater appliqué from plaid fabric. Overlapping as necessary, arrange appliqués on one end of chairback cover; fuse in place. Tie gold ribbon into a bow; glue to dog. Glue ornament to point of chairback cover.

MEDALLION STOCKINGS
(Shown on page 24)

 For each stocking, you will need ½ yd. each of red fabric for stocking and fabric for lining, sewing thread, 3½" x 14½" piece of black-and-white checked fabric for cuff, 6" x 14½" piece of blue plaid fabric for cuff lining, 6" of ⅝"w red grosgrain ribbon for hanger, and a Medallion Ornament with out hanger (page 26).

Match right sides and raw edges and use a ¼" seam allowance for all sewing unless otherwise indicated.

1. Enlarge pattern, page 31, on photocopier 144%; cut out. Matching right sides and short edges, fold fabrics for stocking and lining in half. Using pattern, cut out stocking and lining pieces.
2. Leaving top edge open, sew stocking pieces together. Clip curves; turn stocking right side out. Sew lining pieces together; do not turn.

3. For cuff, matching right sides and one long edge, place cuff and cuff lining together. Sew along long edge. Press seam allowance toward lining. Matching short edges, fold cuff in half; sew short edges together to form a circle. Matching raw edges, fold cuff in half with lining inside cuff (cuff lining will extend 1" below cuff); press.
4. Place cuff inside stocking with right side of cuff facing wrong side of stocking. With seamline of cuff matching heel side seamline of stocking, match raw edges and sew cuff and stocking together. Trim seam allowance. Fold cuff down over stocking
5. For hanger, fold ribbon in half to form a loop. Matching raw ends of loop to top of stocking at heel side seamline, tack hanger in place inside stocking.
6. Place lining inside stocking. Hand sew pressed edge of lining to seam allowance of cuff; press.
7. Glue medallion to stocking.

SMALL TOPIARY PLACECARD
(Shown on page 25)

For each placecard, you will need floral foam, small brass container (we used a 2½"w x 2¾"h container), 4½" long twig for trunk, 2½" dia. plastic foam ball, hot glue gun, Spanish moss, artificial greenery with berries, 1" x 2⅜" piece of card stock, 2¼" lengths each of ½"w ribbon and narrow gold trim, and a permanent pen.

1. Cut plastic foam to fit in container. Insert twig in foam. Insert remaining end of twig into ball.
2. Glue moss around ball and top of foam. Glue greenery around ball.
3. Glue ribbon and trim lengths around one end of card piece. Write name on card. Place card on container; glue to secure if necessary.

STITCHED CLOCK ORNAMENTS
(page 27)

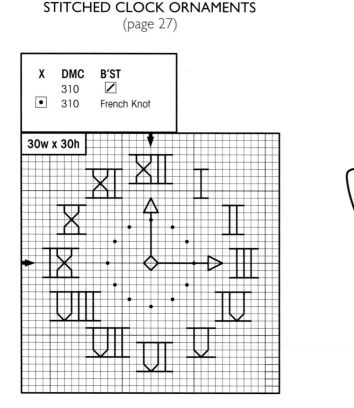

X	DMC	B'ST
	310	◢
⊡	310	French Knot

30w x 30h

SCOTTIE BOXES
(page 27)

SCOTTIE CHAIRBACK COVER
(page 29)

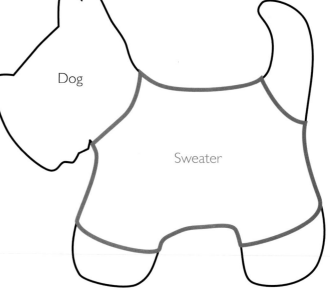

Dog

Sweater

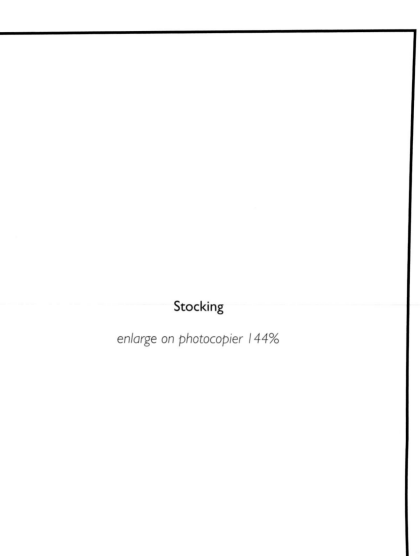

Stocking

enlarge on photocopier 144%

We predict a blizzard of smiles when you "build" these snowmen using odds and ends rescued from the trash can. You'll find more than a dozen great ideas for transforming everyday toss-aways into the most festive of treasures, so start saving your bags and bottles now to finish in time for Christmas! Complete instructions, including those for the glowing *Snowman Lights* pictured below, begin on page 36.

You Can Build a Snowman!

Recycled cheer radiates from every branch of this **You Can Build a Snowman Tree** (page 36)! The friendly **Soda-Bottle Snowmen** (page 38), **Slender Snowmen** (page 37), and **Bubble Wrap Snowmen** (page 37) are all dapperly dressed for the season in their top hats and mufflers. Painted on soda cans, the **Snow Scene Ornaments** (page 37) feature a frosty fellow with his redbird friend, while the **Brown Bag Snowman Ornaments** (page 36) and the **Light Bulb Snowman Ornaments** (page 36) offer their festive smiles. There are even sweet **Snow Angels** (page 38) floating nearby on cardboard wings. Finally, **Carrot Icicles** (page 37) join with the **Packing Peanut Garland** (page 36) and **Snowflake Ornaments** (page 36) to round out the twice-treasured decorations on this terrific tree!

Who's that raiding the pantry? The three little snowmen of the **Carrot-Can Crew** (page 38), that's who! Placed to catch a visitor's eye, these "chilled" chuckle-getters are a winsome conversation piece.

Let these cool characters help with your Yuletide display! In their bright bubble-wrap vests, they're ready to spread seasonal cheer. No one will ever guess this handy **Frosty Fellows Card Holder** (page 39) began with ordinary soda bottles.

You Can Build a Snowman

*Recycling at Christmas? Of course! It's the perfect time of year to show your concern for our world's ecology. There's a jolly blizzard of new-again snowmen on our whimsical **You Can Build a Snowman Tree** (shown on page 33). Torn-fabric bows and purchased garland add crisp touches of color to the evergreen branches. Plastic foam balls wrapped in white plastic bag pieces and secured with chenille stems become no-melt doubles for snowballs. We even used bubble wrap and packing peanuts to make a wintry tree skirt. Follow our easy instructions to create the **Soda-Bottle Snowmen**, **Slender Snowmen**, **Bubble Wrap Snowmen**, and **Snow Scene Ornaments**. But don't stop there! Keep on crafting to complete the **Brown Bag Snowman Ornaments**, **Snow Angels**, **Carrot Icicles**, **Snowflake Ornaments**, and **Packing Peanut Garland**. With these quick-and-easy earth-friendly ideas, you'll have guilt-free fun while making your own merrily "recycled" tree.*

PACKING PEANUT GARLAND
(Shown on page 34)

Recycled items you will need: white foam food trays and packing peanuts

You will also need a drawing compass, decorative-edge craft scissors, craft knife, cutting mat, sharp needle, nylon thread, and a low-temperature glue gun.

1. For each snowflake, use compass to draw a 1¹/₂" dia. circle on foam tray. Use craft scissors to cut out circle. Use craft knife to cut five evenly spaced "V" shapes around circle.
2. Cut a length of thread the desired length for garland; knot one end. Thread peanuts onto thread. Glue snowflakes between peanuts. Knot remaining thread end. Apply glue to knot on each end; allow to dry.

SNOWFLAKE ORNAMENTS
(Shown on page 34)

Recycled item you will need for each ornament: a lid from a 12-oz. frozen juice can

You will also need a hammer, nail, white spray primer, blue spray paint, white paint pen, and 8" of clear nylon thread.

Allow primer and paint to dry after each application.

1. Use hammer and nail to punch a hole close to edge of lid. Spray lid with primer, then blue paint. Use paint pen to draw a snowflake design on lid.

2. For hanger, insert thread through hole; knot ends together.

BROWN BAG SNOWMAN ORNAMENTS
(Shown on page 34)

Recycled items you will need for each ornament: a brown paper bag, two plastic bottle caps for ear muffs, toothbrush, and two black buttons for eyes

You will also need a drawing compass; decorative-edge craft scissors; white and red spray paint; polyester fiberfill; tracing paper; transfer paper; white, orange, and black acrylic paint; paintbrushes; black permanent fine-point marker; hot glue gun; hammer; nail; white spray primer; and 12" of medium-gauge craft wire.

Refer to Painting Techniques, page 157, before beginning project. Allow paint to dry after each application.

1. Use compass to draw two 5" dia. circles on bag. Use craft scissors to cut out circles. Lightly spray paint one side of each circle white.
2. Trace face pattern, page 144, onto tracing paper; use transfer paper to transfer design to white side of one circle. Paint nose orange and eyes, mouth, and details on nose black. Use marker to draw "stitches" along edge of circle.
3. Matching wrong sides and leaving an opening for stuffing, glue circles together along edges. Lightly stuff ornament with fiberfill; glue opening closed.

4. Use hammer and nail to punch a hole in side of each bottle cap. Apply primer to caps. Paint caps red. Use white acrylic paint to lightly spatter paint head and bottle caps.
5. For ear muffs, insert ends of wire through holes in caps; bend ends to secure. Bend wire into a "U" shape. Glue ear muffs and eyes to head.

LIGHT BULB SNOWMAN ORNAMENTS
(Shown on page 34)

Recycled items you will need for each ornament: a standard light bulb and a toddler-size sock for hat

You will also need white spray primer, white matte spray paint, black permanent medium-point marker, white and red paint pens, orange craft foam, low-temperature glue gun, 1" dia. white pom-pom, and 8" of nylon thread.

Allow primer and paint to dry after each application.

1. Apply primer to light bulb. Spray paint bulb white. With base of bulb at top, use marker to draw eyes and mouth, red paint pen to draw hearts for cheeks, and white paint pen to add highlights to eyes.
2. For nose, cut a ³/₈" square from craft foam. Cut square in half diagonally. Glue one half to face for nose; discard remaining half.
3. For hat, fold cuff of sock 1¹/₂" to right side. Arrange hat over base of bulb; glue to secure. Glue pom-pom to tip of hat.
4. For hanger, thread nylon thread through hat; knot ends together.

BUBBLE WRAP SNOWMEN
(Shown on page 34)

Recycled items you will need for each snowman: two white plastic spoons, 2" dia. jar lid, 3½" square of bubble wrap, white foam packing peanuts, and fabric

You will also need white and silver spray paint; black acrylic paint; paintbrush; low-temperature glue gun; white, orange, and black dimensional paint; tracing paper; black craft foam; hole punch; and 12" of floral wire.

Allow paint to dry after each application.

1. For shovel, cut ½" from each end of one spoon. Spray paint shovel silver. Paint handle of shovel black.
2. For body, spray paint lid white. Center lid flat side down on smooth side of bubble wrap. Glue edges of bubble wrap to back of lid. Glue body to back of remaining spoon just below bowl.
3. Use dimensional paint to paint face on back of spoon bowl. Trace hat pattern, page 144, onto tracing paper; cut out. Draw around pattern on craft foam; cut out. Glue hat to head.
4. Glue shovel to body. Glue peanuts to body for arms, legs, hands, and feet. Glue pieces of peanuts to top of hat and in scoop of shovel for snow. For buttons, punch two holes from craft foam; glue to body.
5. Glue a ¼" × 1" strip of fabric across hat for hatband. For hanger, twist wire around neck of snowman; twist ends together. Knot a ½" × 6" strip of fabric around snowman's neck, covering wire.

CARROT ICICLES
(Shown on page 34)

Recycled items you will need for each icicle: a brown paper bag and a rubber band

You will also need tracing paper, white spray primer, orange spray paint, hot glue gun, polyester fiberfill, green raffia, craft stick, glitter textured snow medium, and 6" of clear nylon thread.

Allow primer, paint, and snow medium to dry after each application.

1. Trace carrot pattern, page 143, onto tracing paper; cut out. Draw around pattern on paper bag; cut out. Apply primer to one side of paper piece. Spray paint primed side of paper piece orange. Shape paper piece into a cone; glue overlapped edges together to secure.
2. Stuff carrot with fiberfill. For carrot top, gather several 6" lengths of raffia into a bundle. Use rubber band to secure one end of bundle. Gather top of carrot around bundle, covering rubber band; glue to secure.
3. Use craft stick to apply snow medium to top of carrot. For hanger, glue ends of thread to carrot.

SLENDER SNOWMEN
(Shown on page 34)

Recycled items you will need for each snowman: a toilet paper tube, 3" dia. jar lid, paper towel tube, fabric, and two twigs

You will also need white and black spray paint, 2"w wooden heart, black craft foam, hot glue gun, black permanent medium-point marker, 1⅛" artificial carrot, push pin, and a 1½" artificial redbird.

1. For hat crown, cut a 2" length from toilet paper tube. Spray paint crown, lid, and heart black; allow to dry. For body, spray paint paper towel tube white; allow to dry.
2. For top of hat, draw around one end of crown on craft foam. Cut out circle just inside drawn line; glue along inside edge of one end of crown. For hat brim, center and glue open end of crown on top of lid. For hatband, tear a ½" × 6" strip from fabric; glue around hat.
3. Center and glue hat on one end of body. For feet, glue heart to opposite end of body.
4. For face, use marker to draw eyes and mouth on body. For nose, glue carrot to face.
5. Use push pin to make pilot holes in body for arms. Apply glue to one end

of each twig; insert twigs into holes.
6. For tie, tear a ¾" × 12" strip from fabric. Trim each end to a point. Refer to Fig. 1 and Fig. 2 to knot tie around snowman; glue to secure. Glue bird to arm.

Fig. 1

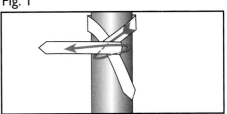

Fig. 2

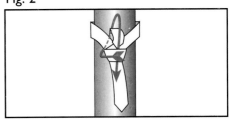

SNOW SCENE ORNAMENTS
(Shown on page 34)

Recycled item you will need for each ornament: a 12-oz. aluminum beverage can

You will also need white spray primer; blue matte spray paint; tracing paper; transfer paper; white, orange, red, blue, and grey acrylic paint; paintbrushes; black permanent fine-point marker; spray sealer; 24" of medium-gauge craft wire; and a hot glue gun.

Allow primer, paint, and sealer to dry after each application.

1. Use both hands to hold can with thumbs below top rim and opening. Using thumbs, press on can to bend top rim down. Turn can upside down and repeat to bend bottom of can in same direction (Fig. 1).

Fig. 1

2. Apply primer to can. Spray paint can blue paint. Trace snow scene pattern, page 143, onto tracing paper. Use transfer paper to transfer design to can.

3. Follow *Painting Techniques*, page 157, to paint design. Use marker to draw over transferred lines. Apply two to three coats of sealer to can.

4. For hanger, leaving 5" at each end of wire straight, curl center of wire around a pencil; remove pencil. Bend wire into a "U" shape. Glue ends of wire to back of can.

SNOW ANGELS
(Shown on page 34)

Recycled items you will need for each angel: a plastic bottle (we used a 1⁷/₈" dia. x 7"h hair spray bottle without lid), toothbrush, knit fabric for hat, fabric for scarf, twigs, three buttons, and narrow ribbon

You will also need white spray primer, white spray paint, tracing paper, corrugated craft cardboard, toothpick, white and orange acrylic paint, paintbrushes, 2" dia. plastic foam ball, whole cloves, low-temperature glue gun, thread, miniature pinecones, hammer, nail, 10" of jute twine, 6" of white chenille stem, and eleven ³/₈" dia. white pom-poms.

Allow primer and paint to dry after each application.

1. For body, apply primer to bottle. Spray paint bottle white.

2. Trace wing pattern, page 144, onto tracing paper; cut out. Draw around pattern on cardboard; cut out. Use white acrylic paint and follow *Spatter Painting*, page 158, to paint wings.

3. For nose, paint 1" of one end of toothpick orange. Cut off orange section; discard remaining portion of toothpick.

4. For head, press ball onto "neck" of body. Push two cloves into head for eyes. Break heads off of five cloves. Insert clove stems into head for mouth. Insert cut end of nose into head.

5. For hat, cut a 4¹/₂" x 6³/₄" piece from fabric. Overlapping short edges

¹/₄", glue short edges together to form a tube. For cuff, turn one edge ³/₈" twice to right side. For fringe, make ³/₄" long clips ¹/₂" apart along opposite edge from cuff. Gather hat below fringe. Knot thread around gathers. Place hat on head; glue to secure. Glue pinecones to cuff.

6. Use hammer and nail to punch holes in bottle for arms. Apply glue to ends of twigs; insert twigs into holes. Glue buttons to front of body. Tie a 1" x 12" piece of fabric around neck for scarf; fringe ends.

7. For hanger, fold twine in half. Glue ends of twine to corrugated side of wings. Glue corrugated side of wings to body.

8. For wreath, shape chenille stem into a circle; twist ends together to secure. Glue pom-poms around circle. Tie an 8" length of ribbon into a bow. Glue bow to wreath. For wreath hanger, fold a 4" length of ribbon over one arm. Glue ribbon ends to back of wreath. Glue hanger to snowman's arm.

SODA-BOTTLE SNOWMEN
(Shown on page 34)

Recycled items you will need for each snowman: two 16-oz. plastic beverage bottles, poster board, assorted buttons, black embroidery floss, fabric, and twigs

You will also need white and black spray paint, one jumbo and one regular craft stick, batting, hot glue gun, utility knife, cutting mat, tracing paper, utility scissors, corrugated craft cardboard, black felt, wooden skewer, orange acrylic paint, paintbrush, two ³/₈" dia. black buttons for eyes, jute twine, miniature pinecones, and 12" of floral wire.

Allow paint to dry after each application.

1. Spray paint one bottle and craft sticks white. Cut a 14" x 22" piece of batting. Wrap batting around painted bottle; glue to secure. Pleating as necessary, glue batting at top and bottom of bottle.

2. For arms, use utility knife to cut one slit through batting and bottle at each side. Insert jumbo craft stick through slits.

3. Trace mitten pattern, page 143, onto tracing paper; cut out. Use pattern to cut four mittens from felt. Glue two mittens together over each end of regular craft stick. Use utility scissors to cut stick in half. Glue one mitten to each arm. Trimming to fit, wrap each arm with batting; glue ends to secure.

4. For hat, use utility knife to cut 1" from bottom of remaining bottle. Trace hat brim pattern, page 143, onto tracing paper; cut out. Draw around pattern on poster board; cut out. Spray paint hat and brim black.

5. Glue hat to brim. For hatband, cut a ¹/₄" x 10" strip from cardboard; glue around hat. Glue three assorted buttons to hatband. Glue hat on snowman.

6. For nose, paint 1" of one end of skewer orange. Cut off orange section; discard remaining portion of skewer. Glue eyes and nose to snowman. Shape and glue 1" length of floss to face for mouth.

7. Knot a ⁷/₈" x 20" strip of fabric around neck for scarf. Fringe ends. Glue twigs together in a bundle. Knot twine around bundle. Glue pinecones over knot in twine. Glue bundle to arm of snowman.

8. For hanger, insert wire through batting at back of snowman; twist ends together to secure.

CARROT-CAN CREW
(Shown on page 35)

Recycled items you will need: an empty can with carrot label, twigs, black aquarium gravel, plastic bottle cap, and artificial evergreen sprigs

For each snowman, you will also need white felt; 5¹/₂"w x 8¹/₂"h piece of batting for tall snowman, 6"w x 6¹/₂"h piece of batting for medium snowman, and 5¹/₂"w x 6"h piece of batting for small snowman; hot glue gun; polyester fiberfill; utility scissors; orange and black acrylic paint; paintbrushes; seam ripper; black spray paint; and black craft foam.

Allow paint to dry after each application.

1. Measure around can; add $1/2$". Cut a piece of felt $2^1/2$"w by the determined measurement. For "icicles," cutting to within $1/2$" of opposite edge, cut uneven "V" shapes along one long edge of felt. Glue straight edge inside top of can. Fold icicles down over can. Spot glue to secure.
2. (Follow Steps 2 and 3 for each snowman body.) Use a $1/2$" seam allowance and sew long edges of one batting piece together to form a tube. Leaving a 2" long tail, work *Running Stitches*, page 158, along one end of tube. Pull thread ends to gather end of tube; knot and trim ends. Turn tube right side out. Leaving $1/2$" at bottom of body unstuffed, stuff snowman with fiberfill; sew opening closed.
3. For each nose, use utility scissors to cut a $1^1/2$" length from twig; paint twig orange. Use seam ripper to make a small hole in snowman for nose. Apply glue to one end of nose and insert into hole. Glue two pieces of gravel to snowman for eyes.
4. For tall snowman, use seam ripper to make a small hole in each side of snowman for arms. Apply glue to one end of each twig and insert into holes. For medium snowman, use seam ripper to make a small hole in one side of snowman for arm. Apply glue to one end of twig and insert into hole.
5. Spray paint bottle cap black. For hat, draw around bottle cap on craft foam. Cut out circle $1/4$" outside drawn line. Glue cap to circle. Glue hat to top of tall snowman.
6. Arrange and glue snowmen and greenery in can.

FROSTY FELLOWS CARD HOLDER
(Shown on page 35)

Recycled items you will need: six 3-liter plastic soda bottles with caps, red T-shirt, brown paper bag, bubble wrap, two 30" long $1/2$" dia. branches, fabric, and buttons

You will also need sand to weight two bottles; utility knife; white,

orange, and green spray paint; batting; hot glue gun; jute twine; whole cloves; straight pins; miniature pinecones; artificial holly pick; and small clothespins.

Allow paint to dry after each application.

1. For each snowman body, remove caps from three bottles; fill one bottle half full with sand and replace cap. Mark around each empty bottle 5" from bottom. Use utility knife to cut tops from bottles along marked lines; discard bottoms. Stack cut bottles on top of sand-filled bottle; push down firmly to secure.
2. Spray paint body white. Cut a 28" × 40" piece of batting. Wrap batting around body twice; glue to secure at sides and bottom. Tuck batting at top into opening at top of body.
3. For each hat, cut a 10" × 20" piece from T-shirt. Use a $1/2$" seam allowance and sew long edges of T-shirt piece together to form a tube. Turn tube right side out. Place hat on snowman and tie twine into a bow around top of hat.
4. For face, glue cloves to snowman for mouth and two buttons to face for eyes. For nose, cut a $2^3/4$" × 4" piece from brown paper bag; roll into a cone. Glue to secure. Trim wide end of cone even. Spray paint nose orange. Cut a hole in face for nose. Apply glue to nose. Insert nose into hole.
5. For each vest, cut a 10" × 22" piece from bubble wrap. Spray paint both sides of vest green. Place vest around snowman; pin to secure. Cutting through all layers, use utility knife to cut a $3/4$"h "X" in each side of body for arms. Insert one branch through "X"s in vest and body. Cut both sides of bottom front of vest at an angle. Glue vest to snowman to secure. Glue buttons to front of vest; remove pins.
6. For scarf, cut a $7/8$" × 36" strip from fabric. Tie scarf around neck of snowman. For bow tie, cut a $2^1/2$" × 10" and a $1/2$" × $1^1/2$" strip from fabric. Fold ends of 10" strip to center back, glue to secure. Pinching center of strip, wrap $1^1/2$" strip around gathers; glue to secure. Glue bow tie to neck of snowman.

7. Glue buttons, pinecones, or holly pick to hat.
8. Cut a 45" length of twine. With twine draping between snowmen, tie ends of twine to snowmen's arms. Use clothespins to hang cards on twine.

SNOWMAN LIGHTS
(Shown on page 32)

Recycled items you will need for each light: a canning jar with lid and band, two black shank buttons, and a toddler-size or adult-size sock

You will also need white and orange acrylic paint, household sponge; paintbrush; black permanent medium-point marker; wire cutters; hot glue gun; tin snips; duct tape; 5-watt electrical wiring harness with socket clip; 5-watt cool-burning light bulb; thread; white, red, and green yarn (optional); $1^1/2$" dia. white pom-pom (optional); and white dimensional paint.

Refer to Painting Techniques, page 157, before beginning project. Allow paint to dry after each application.

1. Use white acrylic paint to sponge paint outside of jar. Paint an orange nose on jar. Use marker to draw mouth and to outline nose and add details to nose.
2. Use wire cutters to remove shanks from buttons. Glue buttons to jar for eyes.
3. Use tin snips to cut a $1^1/8$" dia. hole in jar lid. Cover rough edges with duct tape. Insert socket clip into jar lid. Screw light bulb into socket. Place lid and band on jar.
4. For hat, fold top of sock to right side to form cuff. Place hat over jar. If fringe is desired on hat, cut toe of sock open and make clips along toe. Use thread to gather hat below fringe.
5. If desired, refer to *Making a Pom-pom*, page 157, and use yarn to make a 4" dia. pom-pom. Glue yarn pom-pom or white pom-pom to tip of hat.
6. Use dimensional paint to add highlights to eyes and snowflakes to hat if desired.

Sportsman's Holiday

*H*ere's your license to celebrate the holiday season in sportsman style! You don't need any fancy gewgaws to create this "roughin'-it" Christmas — just a little crafting know-how and a sporting attitude. The **Great Outdoors Wreath** pictured here is just one of the rugged field-and-stream trophies you'll find to enliven a hunting lodge or accent an angler's quarters. Instructions begin on page 44.

*M*ake a Christmas tree forest for an outdoorsman! This **Sportsman's Holiday Tree** (page 44) is actually four assorted-size pines loaded with back-to-nature decorations like the warm little **Long John Ornaments** (page 45) made from toddler-size socks and the **Boot Ornaments** (page 44) made from camouflage flannel. For the fishing enthusiast, the painted **Soda-Can Trout** (page 45) celebrate the one that didn't get away. The bright **Flannel Garland** (page 44) adds a warm touch of cool-weather color. Finally, little wooden **"Gone Fishing" and "Gone Hunting" Signs** (page 45) announce your sportsman's favorite leisure-time pursuits.

*T*rail mix, a compass, a pocket knife — just imagine the useful little treats you can tuck inside a camouflage **Boot Stocking** (page 44). This faux footwear is one-size-fits-all fun!

It's no fish story! The **Fisherman's Frame** *(page 46) and* **Shotgun Shell Frame** *(page 45) make great gifts for proud outdoorsmen. What better ways to display memories of a prize catch or a day spent with man's best friend?*

Sportsman's Holiday

*For a look as big as all outdoors, one tree just isn't enough! Our **Sportsman's Holiday Tree** (shown on page 41) is actually a grouping of four slender pines. Lengths of whitewashed fishnet tucked among the branches make the perfect backdrop for our sportsman-themed projects, such as the **Long John Ornaments** and **Boot Ornaments**. A bamboo fishing pole takes the place of a tree topper as it extends above the trees, and the "bobbers" are created by simply dipping red glass ornaments into white acrylic paint. Adding to the fishing theme are the **Soda-Can Trout** with their realistic rainbow speckles. **Flannel Garland** winds about the limbs, and **"Gone Fishing" and "Gone Hunting" Signs** are prominently posted. Purchased lantern ornaments go great with directional compasses, artificial antlers, and duck decoys. Empty shotgun shell casings are hung here and there on the branch tips. A warm wool blanket and a length of plaid flannel make the perfect skirt for this Christmas tree forest.*

BOOT STOCKING
(Shown on page 43)

For each stocking, you will need tracing paper, 14" x 24" piece each of tan fabric and fabric for lining, paper-backed fusible web, camouflage print flannel, brown fabric, brown thread, stabilizer, eyelet tool, five brown eyelets, brown shoe string, black craft foam, and low-temperature glue gun.

Match right sides and raw edges and use a ¹/₄" seam allowance for all sewing unless otherwise indicated.

1. Aligning arrows and dashed lines, trace stocking top and stocking bottom patterns, page 47, onto tracing paper. For seam allowance, draw a second line ¹/₄" outside first line. Cut out pattern along outer line.
2. Matching right sides and short edges, fold fabric pieces in half. Using pattern, cut stocking pieces from tan fabric and fabric for lining.
3. Using patterns, page 46, follow *Making Appliqués*, page 156, to make one A appliqué from flannel and one each of B and C appliqués from brown fabric. Refer to Stocking Diagram, page 46 to arrange and fuse appliqués to right side of one stocking piece (front). Leaving outer raw edges of stocking unstitched, use brown thread and follow *Machine Appliqué*, page 156, to stitch over raw edges of appliqués and add detail lines.
4. Beginning 1¹/₄" from top edge of stocking front, mark placement for eyelets at 1¹/₂" intervals along appliqué B. Use eyelet tool to insert eyelets. Tacking each end of shoe string on wrong side and wrapping

over raw edge, lace shoe string through eyelets.
5. Leaving top edges open, sew stocking pieces together; clip curves and turn right side out.
6. For hanger, cut a 2" x 8" piece from brown fabric. Press long edges ¹/₂" to wrong side. Matching wrong sides and long edges, press in half. Stitch along pressed edges. Fold hanger in half to form a loop. Matching raw edges, tack loop inside stocking at heel seam.
7. Leaving top edges open and a 2" opening along heel seam, sew lining pieces together; clip curves. Do not turn right side out.
8. Matching top edges and seams, place stocking inside lining. Sew top edges together. Pull stocking through opening in lining. Turn lining right side out. Sew opening closed. Insert lining into stocking.
9. Trace sole pattern, page 47, onto tracing paper. Draw around pattern on craft foam; cut out. Glue straight edge of sole along bottom back of stocking.

FLANNEL GARLAND
(Shown on page 42)

You will need plaid flannel, safety pin, and jute rope.

1. For a six-foot length of garland, cut a twelve-foot strip of flannel 3¹/₂"w, piecing as necessary.
2. Matching right sides and long edges, use a ¹/₄"w seam allowance to sew long raw edges together to make a tube; turn right side out.
3. Cut a 6-foot length of rope; knot one end. Attach safety pin to opposite end. Using pin as a guide and gathering flannel evenly, thread rope through tube. Remove pin and knot remaining end of rope to secure.

BOOT ORNAMENTS
(Shown on page 42)

For each ornament, you will need tracing paper, camouflage print flannel, red checked flannel, silver acrylic paint, cap without clip from pen or marker, paper towel, black embroidery floss, and an embroidery needle.

1. Trace stocking and cuff patterns, page 146, onto tracing paper. With right sides together, fold camouflage flannel in half. Using patterns, cut stocking pieces from camouflage flannel. Cut two cuffs from red checked flannel.
2. For each cuff, press short edges of cuff piece ¹/₂" to wrong side. Matching wrong sides and pressed edges, press each cuff piece in half. Insert top edge of stocking pieces into fold of cuffs. Stitch along pressed edges. Matching right sides and leaving top open, sew stocking pieces together. Clip curves and turn right side out.
3. For each "eyelet," dip open end of cap into paint. Blotting on towel as necessary, press cap on stocking to make six eyelets on each side of stocking.
4. Beginning and ending at top eyelet and leaving 6" at each end of floss, use needle to lace floss through eyelets. Tie floss ends into a bow.
5. For hanger, cut a 2" x 8" piece from red checked flannel. Press long edges ¹/₂" to wrong side. Matching wrong sides and long edges, press hanger in half. Stitch along pressed edges. Fold hanger in half to form a loop. Matching raw edges, tack loop inside stocking at heel seam.

"GONE FISHING" AND "GONE HUNTING" SIGNS
(Shown on page 42)

For each sign, you will need a $3^3/4$" x 5" oval unfinished wooden sign with hanger, wood stain, soft cloth, acrylic paint, paintbrushes, tracing paper, transfer paper, black permanent fine-point marker, clear acrylic matte spray sealer, and 16" medium-gauge craft wire.

Refer to Painting Techniques, page 157, before beginning project. Allow paint and sealer to dry after each application.

1. Remove hanger from sign. Apply stain to sign. Wipe with soft cloth. Paint side edge of sign.
2. Trace desired pattern, page 145, onto tracing paper. Use transfer paper to transfer design to sign. Paint design. Use marker to outline and add details to design.
3. Apply two to three coats of sealer to sign.
4. Leaving 2" at each end uncurled, wrap wire around pencil; remove pencil. Insert ends into holes for hanger in sign. Bend wire ends to secure.

SODA-CAN TROUT
(Shown on page 42)

For each trout, you will need utility scissors; 12-oz. aluminum beverage can; green and black spray paint; spray primer; tracing paper; light-colored craft foam; decorative-edge craft scissors; white, yellow, orange, pink, green, tan, brown, and black acrylic paint; natural sponge; paintbrush; clear acrylic matte spray sealer; push pin; 9" of black craft wire; and household cement.

Allow primer, paint, sealer, and household cement to dry after each application.

1. Use utility scissors to cut top from can. For mouth, squeeze opening into an oval shape. Apply primer to inside and outside of can. Spray paint inside of can black.
2. Trace pectoral fin, dorsal fin, and tail patterns, page 46, onto tracing paper; cut out. Draw around pectoral fin twice and dorsal fin and tail fin once on craft foam; cut out. Use craft scissors to trim $1/8$" from curved edges of dorsal fin and tail fin. Spray paint both sides of pectoral fins and outside of can green.
3. Paint rim of can, pectoral fin, and tail fin yellow. Follow *Sponge Painting*, page 157, to paint curved edges of dorsal fin and tail fin green. Use paintbrush to paint yellow and orange details on both sides of pectoral fins. Glue dorsal fin and tail fin to can.
4. Sponge paint "belly" of fish yellow. Sponge paint area under mouth orange and a pink strip along each side of fish. Use end of paintbrush to paint brown, tan and orange dots on sides of fish. Paint smaller orange dots over several brown dots. Paint eyes; add yellow highlights.
5. Glue pectoral fins to sides of fish. Apply two to three coats of sealer to fish.
6. For hanger, use push pin to make holes at top and bottom of mouth. Thread wire through holes and twist to secure.

LONG JOHN ORNAMENTS
(Shown on page 42)

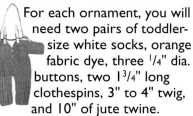

For each ornament, you will need two pairs of toddler-size white socks, orange fabric dye, three $1/4$" dia. buttons, two $1^3/4$" long clothespins, 3" to 4" twig, and 10" of jute twine.

1. Follow manufacturer's instructions to dye socks orange.
2. For long johns, flatten two socks with heel at back. Sew socks together, side by side, from toe seam to cuff ribbing. For sleeves, cut cuffs from remaining socks, discard toe sections. Pinch a pleat in each side of long johns to shape shoulders. Insert cut ends of sleeves into pleats; stitch in place.
3. Sew buttons to front of long johns. Use clothespins to fasten long johns to twig. For hanger, knot ends of twine around ends of twig.

GREAT OUTDOORS WREATH
(Shown on page 40)

You will need a 24" dia. artificial evergreen wreath with pinecones, 2" dia. plastic foam balls, 10" squares of camouflage flannel, rubber bands, hot glue gun, artificial deer antlers, six-foot length of Flannel Garland (page 44), empty shotgun shell casings, and a duck decoy.

1. For each camouflage ornament, wrap flannel square around foam ball, gather edges of square, and secure with rubber band.
2. Arrange and glue ornaments, antlers, and garland to wreath. Gluing to secure, insert casings over branch ends of wreath. Position and glue decoy in wreath.

SHOTGUN SHELL FRAME
(Shown on page 43)

You will need wooden frame, decoupage glue, foam brush, hunting motifs from sporting magazines, hot glue gun, cardboard, craft knife, and empty shotgun shell casings.

1. Cut motifs from magazines. Use foam brush to apply decoupage glue to wrong sides of motifs. Position and smooth motifs onto frame; allow to dry. Allowing to dry after each application, apply two to three coats of decoupage glue over motifs.
2. Place frame on cardboard. Draw around opening and outside edges of frame. Cut out opening along drawn lines. Cut outer edges of cardboard $1/2$" outside drawn line. Hot glue cardboard to back of frame. Using craft knife to trim casings as necessary, hot glue casings to cardboard along edges of frame.

FISHERMAN'S FRAME
(Shown on page 43)

You will need an unfinished wooden frame, green acrylic paint, paintbrush, decoupage glue, foam brush, fish motifs from sporting magazines, hot glue gun, and a 14" miniature fishing rod with lure.

1. Paint frame green; allow to dry. Cut desired motifs from magazines. Use foam brush to apply decoupage glue to wrong sides of motifs. Position and smooth motifs onto frame; allow to dry. Allowing to dry after each application, apply two to three coats of decoupage glue over motifs.
2. Hot glue fishing rod to frame. Hot glue lure to reel.

BOOT STOCKING
(page 44)

Stocking Diagram

SODA-CAN TROUT
(page 45)

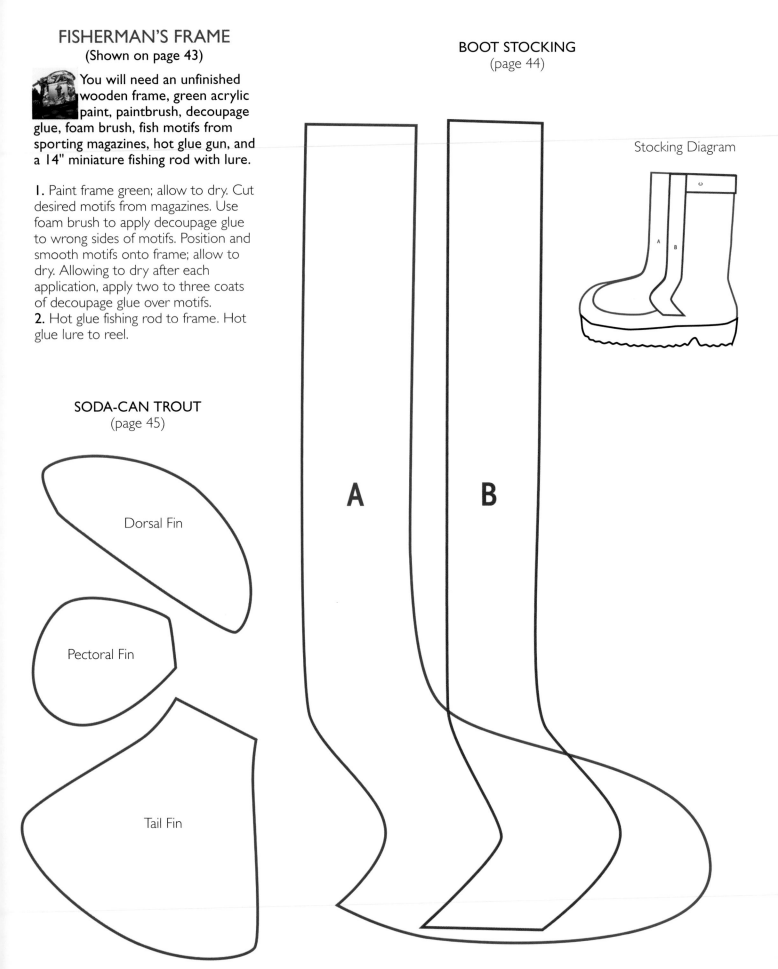

Dorsal Fin

Pectoral Fin

Tail Fin

A

B

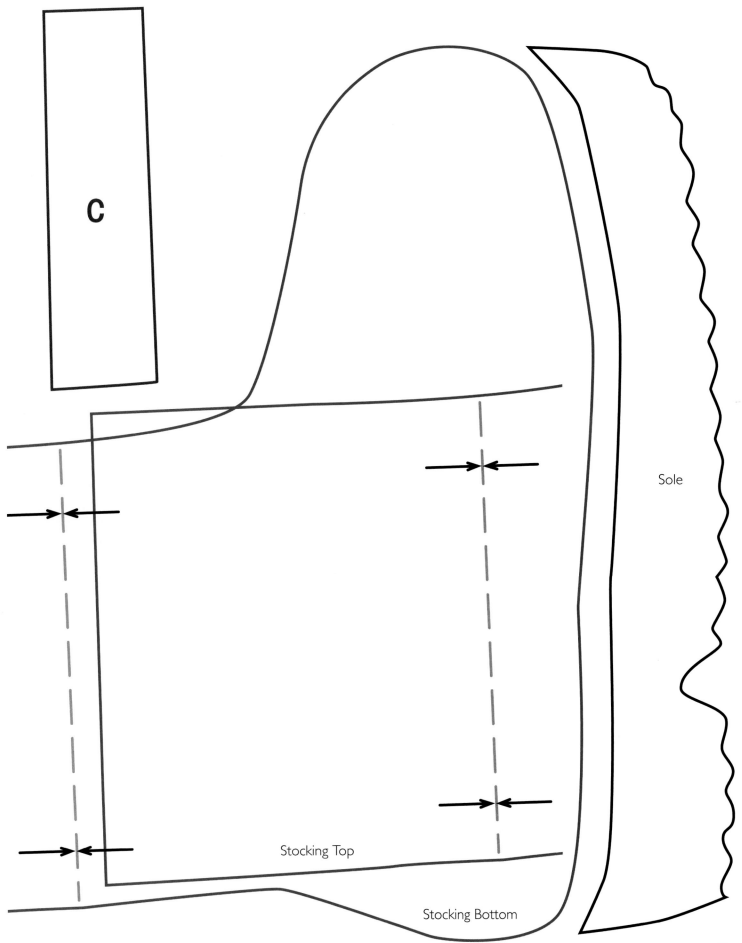

C

Sole

Stocking Top

Stocking Bottom

47

Santa's Workshop

What a magical sight! Busy elves, mischievous and merry, are having a wonderful time preparing for Christmas…with toys scattered everywhere, from table to tree and from mantel to door. This **Elf Shelf Sitter** is a cheerful little fellow, just taking a break from the hustle and bustle. He's surrounded by round glass ornaments with dimensional paint embellishments — so easy to create! Instructions for the elf and many more magical projects begin on page 54.

*W*hat a whirl of activity there is on this **Santa's Workshop Tree** (page 54)! With its transportable red wagon base and a scattering of choo-choo train and airplane ornaments, it's an evergreen on the go. Little tan teddies ride in wooden wagons, coasting past brightly wrapped packages tied with cheerful bows. Freckle-face **Elf Ornaments** (page 54), dressed in felt finery, hold baskets of colorful sweets. Carefully addressed to the head elf himself, the crayoned **Letters to Santa** (page 54) are easy to make.

Let our "a-door-able" greeter present a friendly face to your holiday guests! *Elliot the Elf* (page 57) gives a welcoming smile as he offers a bow-tied bag of Christmas gifts.

*S*itting contentedly in a purchased miniature easy chair, a dapper **Stuffed Santa** (page 55) knows the best way to supervise his elves! Cut from soft upholstery vinyl, the bag of toys in front of the little tree is made just like the tree topper shown opposite and tied with a drapery tieback.

Chock-full of tiny gifts, the **Santa's Bag Tree Topper** (page 54) combines with a peppermint-striped bow to make the perfect finale for a lively evergreen! A cute teddy bear snuggles up to our **Letter to Santa Pillow** (page 54). The cozy cushion is bedecked with holly sprigs and tassels to brighten a corner with Christmas cheer.

Santa's Workshop

*This little evergreen is a fairyland of children's Christmas wishes! Our **Santa's Workshop Tree** (shown on page 49) plays host to over a dozen tiny teddy bears and red wagons. Spreading seasonal cheer, **Elf Ornaments** hold baskets full of candy. The branches are also bedecked with satin ornaments, tinsel garland, and lots of decorative packages that you can either make or buy. Complete with reindeer postage stamps, **Letters to Santa** look ready for an airmail trip to the North Pole. And the **Santa's Bag Tree Topper** is an easy-to-make sack filled with wonderful miniature toys. After all this playful merriment, our tree wouldn't be complete without its red wagon base!*

LETTER TO SANTA PILLOW
(Shown on page 53)

You will need two 13" x 17" pieces of red velvet fabric, 5" x 6¹/₂" piece of clear vinyl, ³/₈"w wired ribbon, craft wire, twelve ³/₄" silk holly leaves, four ¹/₂" dia. jingle bells, four 3" long red tassels, polyester fiberfill, and one Letter to Santa (this page).

1. Cut two 6¹/₂" lengths and two 13" lengths of ribbon. Stitch one 6¹/₂" length of ribbon along each long edge of vinyl. For window, center vinyl at center on right side of one velvet piece. Matching ends with long edges of velvet piece, stitch 13" ribbon lengths to velvet piece along short edges of window. Leaving one long edge of window open (top), stitch remaining long edge to velvet.
2. Cut a 1¹/₃ yd. length of ribbon. Use ribbon and follow *Making a Bow*, page 157, to make a bow with eight 4" loops. Stitch bow to top left corner of window. Stitch three leaves and one bell at each corner of window.
3. Matching right sides and leaving an opening for turning, stitch velvet pieces together. Turn pillow right side out. Stuff pillow with fiberfill; stitch opening closed. Stitch one tassel at each corner of pillow. Arrange and tack streamers of bow to pillow as desired.
4. Insert one Letter to Santa in vinyl window on pillow.

LETTERS TO SANTA
(Shown on page 50)

For each letter, you will need crayons, 4" x 5³/₄" white envelope, photocopy of stamp design (page 58), and a craft glue stick.

1. Use crayon to address envelope to "Santa" at the "North Pole" and write return address name.
2. Cut out stamp design. Use crayons to color stamp. Glue stamp to envelope.

SANTA'S BAG TREE TOPPER
(Shown on page 53)

You will need a 10" x 23" piece of red velvet fabric, pinking shears, tissue paper, 4" x 3" x 4" block of plastic foam, assorted small toys, miniature garland, artificial candy, 16-gauge craft wire, wire cutters, hot glue gun, clear tape, and ¹/₈" dia. decorative cord.

1. Matching right sides and short edges, fold fabric in half; finger press folded edge (bottom of bag). Using a ¹/₂" seam allowance, stitch sides of fabric together. Use pinking shears to trim top of bag.
2. To make a flat bottom on bag, match each side seam with fold line at bottom of bag; sew across each corner 2" from point (Fig. 1). Turn bag right side out.

Fig. 1

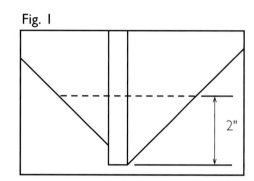

3. Stuff tissue paper in bottom of bag, then place foam block in bag. Arrange toys, garland, and candy in top of bag. Use wire, glue, or tape to secure toys in place. Gather top of bag loosely around toys. Use cord to tie a bow around gathers to secure.
4. Thread a 10" length of wire through back of bag. Use wire to attach bag to top of tree.

ELF ORNAMENTS
(Shown on page 50)

For each ornament, you will need a hot glue gun; two chenille stems for arms; one craft stick for body; cotton batting; craft knife; cutting mat; 2¹/₂" long plastic egg; tracing paper; transfer paper; ¹/₂" dia. wooden button for nose; white, flesh, dark pink, brown, and black acrylic paint; paintbrushes; black permanent fine-point marker; cotton swab; pink cosmetic blush; red and green felt; pinking shears; hot glue gun; drawing compass; ¹/₈"w red-and-white polka-dot satin ribbon; 4mm red bead; heavy-duty green thread; red embroidery floss; 3" dia. basket with handle; artificial "sugar-coated" candy garland; ¹/₂"w red-and-white polka-dot grosgrain ribbon; 16-gauge craft wire; and wire cutters.

Refer to Painting Techniques, page 157, before beginning project. Allow paint to dry after each application.

1. For arms and body, glue center of chenille stems 1" from one end of craft stick forming a "T" shape; twist ends of stems together to strengthen arms. Wrap 1" wide strips of batting around arms and craft stick below arms until body is desired size; glue ends of batting to secure.
2. For head, leaving small end of egg protruding forward for "chin," cut a small opening at bottom back of small end of egg large enough for craft stick to slide through. Leaving 1/2" between arms and head for neck, slide end of craft stick through opening; glue to secure. Arrange and glue nose to face. Paint nose, head, and neck flesh.
3. Paint face. Use cotton swab to apply pink blush across cheeks, nose, and chin.
4. Trace patterns, pages 58 and 59, onto tracing paper; cut out. Use patterns to cut four mittens from red felt and use pinking shears to cut one jacket from green felt.
5. For hat, refer to Hat Diagram, page 58, and measurements in green to cut hat from green felt. Use pinking shears to trim cuff edge of hat. Use a 1/2" seam allowance to stitch back seam of hat. Turn hat right side out; fold cuff of hat up 1/2". Place hat on head; spot glue to secure.
6. For mittens, leaving cuff of mittens open, match two mitten pieces together and stitch along edges. Glue mittens to ends of arms.
7. For jacket, use a 1/4" seam allowance to stitch arm and side seams of jacket. Use pinking shears to cut center front of jacket open. Fit jacket on elf. Tie heavy-duty thread around jacket sleeve over mittens to secure. Overlap front of jacket. Use floss and work *Running Stitches*, page 158, to secure overlap.
8. For collar, use compass to draw a 2 1/2" dia. circle on red felt; use pinking shears to cut out circle. To "fringe" collar, use scissors to cut 1/4" long slits between each point on collar. Cut back opening from outer edge to center of collar; cut an opening at center of collar large enough to fit around neck. Tie a 10" length of 1/8"w

ribbon into a bow. Glue bow to collar; glue bead to knot of bow.
9. Arrange and glue elf's mittens to handle of basket. Arrange and glue garland in basket. Tie 1/2"w ribbon into a bow around handle of basket.
10. For hanger, wrap and twist a 10" length of wire around elf's neck; twist ends together.

ELF SHELF SITTER
(Shown on page 48)

You will need red and green felt, pinking shears, hot glue gun, one Elf Ornament (page 54) without hanger, tracing paper, polyester fiberfill, and two 6" chenille stem pieces.

1. For each leg, cut a 3" x 6" piece from green felt; use pinking shears to trim short edges. Matching long edges, fold felt piece in half. Use a 1/4" seam allowance to stitch long edges together. Turn leg right side out.
2. With seam at back, glue one end of each leg 1/2" above inside bottom edge of back of jacket.
3. For boots, trace pattern, page 58, onto tracing paper; cut out. Using pattern, cut four boot pieces from red felt. Leaving top straight edges of felt open, match two boots together and stitch along edges. Lightly stuff boots with fiberfill.
4. Fold each chenille stem into a "V" shape. Glue ends of one chenille stem 1 1/2" into top of boot; repeat for remaining boot. Insert top of each boot 1/2" into each leg; glue to secure.

STUFFED SANTA
(Shown on page 52)

You will need a Crafts, Etc!® 4"h plastic Santa face (with glasses) and 2" long plastic doll hands; masking tape, spackling, and 2"w gold doll glasses (optional); white, flesh, and pink acrylic paint; paintbrushes; fabric marking pen; pair of men-size white tube socks (ours measure approx. 21" long); polyester fiberfill; rubber band; white heavy-duty thread; tracing paper; red fabric; red sewing thread; straight pins; red

embroidery floss; three 3/4" dia. black buttons; 1" x 23" strip of black vinyl fabric; 1/16" dia. hole punch; 1" square gold belt buckle; white artificial fur; one pair of 3"h shiny black doll boots; hot glue gun; Wavy Locks™ platinum doll hair; 2"w gold doll glasses (optional), and a small artificial holly sprig with berries.

Allow paint to dry after each application. Use hot glue unless otherwise indicated. Match right sides and use a 1/4" seam allowance and a double strand of heavy-duty thread for all stitching unless otherwise indicated.

1. Remove plastic glasses from Santa face. (If gold glasses are desired, apply a piece of masking tape to wrong side of face covering hole in face for glasses. Fill hole with spackling; allow to dry.)
2. Paint face and hands flesh. Paint mustache, eyebrows, and whites of eyes white. Lightly paint nose, cheeks, and mouth pink.
3. (*Note:* Refer to Diagram A, page 56, for Steps 3 and 4.) Use fabric marking pen to mark sock. For body, stuff sock with fiberfill to body stitching line (indicated by dashed line). Wrap rubber band twice around neck (indicated by blue line). Form body as desired. Stitch across body line.
4. For legs, refer to Diagram A to cut remaining portion of sock (indicated by red line). Whipstitch along inside raw edge of each leg. Lightly stuff each leg to knee stitching lines; stitch across knee lines. Lightly stuff remainder of each leg with fiberfill; stitch openings closed.
5. Refer to Diagram B, page 56, to cut arms from second sock. For each arm, whipstitch long raw edges of arm together. Lightly stuff arms. Turn raw edge of arm opening under 1/2". Work *Running Stitches*, page 158, along edge of opening. For each hand, apply craft glue around edge of wrist and insert hand into arm opening. Pull thread ends to tighten opening around indentation in wrist; knot and trim thread ends. Allow to dry.
6. Stitch arms to body near neck, making sure thumbs face forward and palms face body (Fig. 1).

Fig. 1

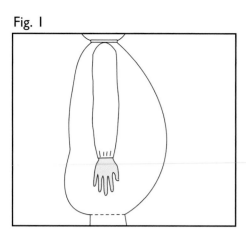

7. For Santa's clothes, refer to *Making Patterns*, page 156, and trace patterns, pages 59 and 148 - 151, onto tracing paper; cut out. Cut one jacket back piece, two jacket front pieces (one in reverse), two sleeve pieces, two pant pieces, and one hat piece from red fabric.

8. For jacket, stitch jacket front and jacket back together at shoulder seams.

9. For each sleeve, pin one sleeve to jacket arm opening (Fig. 2); stitch in place.

Fig. 2

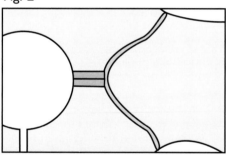

10. Stitch jacket front and jacket back together along sleeve and side seams (Fig. 3). Press neck of jacket $1/4$" to wrong side twice and stitch in place. Turn jacket right side out; press.

Fig. 3

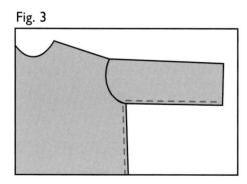

11. Press opening edges of jacket $1/2$" to wrong side; use floss to sew buttons along one pressed edge.

12. Referring to Fig. 4, stitch pant pieces together from waist to crotch. Referring to Fig. 5, align seam at waist and raw edges of each leg; stitch in place. Turn pants right side out and press. For belt, cut one end of vinyl into a point. Use hole punch to punch several holes for belt fastener. Attach belt buckle to belt.

Fig. 4

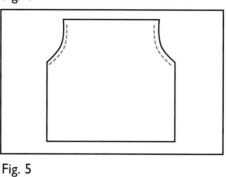

Fig. 5

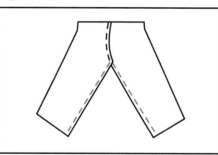

13. Matching right sides, fold hat in half lengthwise. Stitch back seam of hat; turn hat right side out.

14. For fur trim, measure around jacket bottom, each sleeve opening, top of each boot, and bottom edge of hat; add $1/2$" to each measurement. Cut pieces from fur 2"w by the determined measurements. Overlap long edges of each fur strip $1/2$" to form a tube; glue to secure. With overlap at center back of each tube and overlapping ends at back, glue fur tubes in place.

15. For ball on hat, trace pattern, page 148, onto tracing paper; cut out. Use pattern to cut circle from fur. Work *Running Stitches*, page 158, along edges of circle. Tucking edges to inside, pull thread ends to gather fur piece into a ball; knot and trim thread ends. Stitch ball to tip of hat.

16. Place pants on body, spot glue to secure. Insert each leg into top of one boot; glue to secure. Overlapping front of jacket, place jacket on body; glue to secure. If desired, stuff jacket with additional fiberfill. Place belt around jacket; glue to secure.

17. Glue face to front of head. Arrange and glue hair to head and face for hair, beard, moustache, and eyebrows. Replace glasses on face (or place gold glasses on face and glue to secure if hole has been covered). Lightly stuff hat with fiberfill; arrange and glue hat on head. Glue holly and berries to hat.

Diagram A

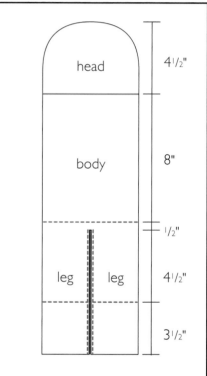

Diagram B

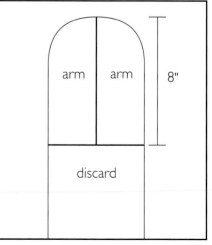

ELLIOT THE ELF
(Shown on page 51)

You will need an 8" long papier-mâché egg; 21" of 5/8" dia. dowel; utility knife; white spray primer; 15" long cardboard fabric bolt; 24" of wired cording; peach craft foam; tracing paper; transfer paper; hot glue gun; craft knife; cutting mat; 1" dia. wooden button for nose; white, flesh, pink, red, brown, and black acrylic paint; paintbrushes; black permanent fine-point marker; cosmetic sponge wedge; 3" x 28" piece of red felt; green felt; high-loft cotton batting; polyester fiberfill; child-size green mittens; awl; 19" x 24" piece of red velvet; filler for sack (we used packing peanuts); pinking shears; hot glue gun; 1⅞"w red-and-white stripe wired satin ribbon; heavy-duty green thread; red embroidery floss; 2" dia. jingle bell; 3" x 4" x 8" plastic foam block; artificial greenery (we used pine boughs with small pinecones, evergreen boughs, and holly with berries); tinsel garland; miniature toys; assorted small boxes, wrapping paper, and ribbons for presents; 30" of 1"w green grosgrain ribbon; 19-gauge craft wire; and wire cutters.

Refer to Painting Techniques, page 157, before beginning project. Allow paint to dry after each application.

1. For head, leaving small end of egg protruding forward for "chin," cut a small opening at bottom back of small end of egg large enough for dowel to slide through. Insert 2" of dowel through opening; glue to secure.
2. (*Note:* Refer to Fig. 1 for Steps 2, 3, and 7.) Cut an opening at center of bolt end large enough for dowel to slide through. Leaving 4" of dowel for neck, insert remaining end of dowel through bolt.

Fig. 1

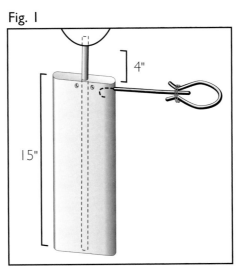

3. For hanger, poke two holes through bolt 1½" from top, 2" apart at center (neck should be between holes). Thread cord ends through holes from front to back; knot ends together.
4. Trace ear pattern, page 58, onto tracing paper; cut out. Draw around pattern twice on craft foam; cut out.
5. Paint neck, head, nose, and ears flesh.
6. Trace eyes pattern, page 58, onto tracing paper. Use transfer paper to transfer eyes to head. Arrange and glue nose on face and ears to sides of head. Paint eyes. Use cosmetic sponge to apply pink blush to cheeks, nose, and chin. Paint brown "freckles" and a dark pink mouth, highlighted with white.
7. For each arm, shape one end of a 20" length of 19-gauge wire into a hook shape and work end through bolt at shoulders. For each hand, fold a 10" length of 19-gauge wire in half. Place ends over opposite end of arm. Wrap ends with floral wire and secure with glue. Wrap shoulders, arms, and hands with batting until desired plumpness is achieved.
8. For jacket, cut a 30" x 56" piece from green felt. Matching long edges, fold felt piece in half. Matching short edges, fold in half again. Refer to Jacket Diagram, this page, and use pinking shears to cut out jacket. Refer to Step 7 of Elf Ornaments, page 54, to stitch jacket. With opening at back, place jacket on elf. Lightly stuff mittens with fiberfill. Place mittens on hands. Gather sleeve of jacket around wrist

of mitten; secure gathers with heavy-duty thread.
9. For collar, use pinking shears to cut two 3" x 12" strips of red felt. For fringe, use scissors to cut 1" long slits 3/8" apart along one long edge of each strip. Matching edges, place strips together. Overlapping short ends at back, wrap collar around neck; glue in place.
10. For sack, using velvet and sewing 5" from point, follow Steps 1 and 2 of Santa's Bag Tree Topper, page 54, to make sack.
11. Use wire, glue, and floral picks to arrange packages, toys and greenery on foam block. Place block on "chest" of elf. Overlapping ends at front, tightly wrap grosgrain ribbon around elf and block. Insert greening pins through overlapped area of ribbon and into block to secure block to elf. Place elf in sack. Pull sack over block and tie wired ribbon into a bow around top of bag.
12. Tack mittens to sides of sack.
13. For hat, refer to Hat Diagram, page 58, and using measurements in red, refer to Step 5 of Elf Ornaments, page 54, to make hat. Place hat on elf's head.

Jacket Diagram

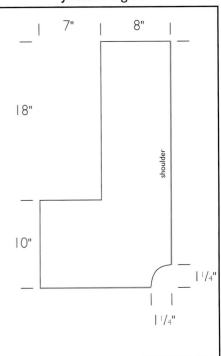

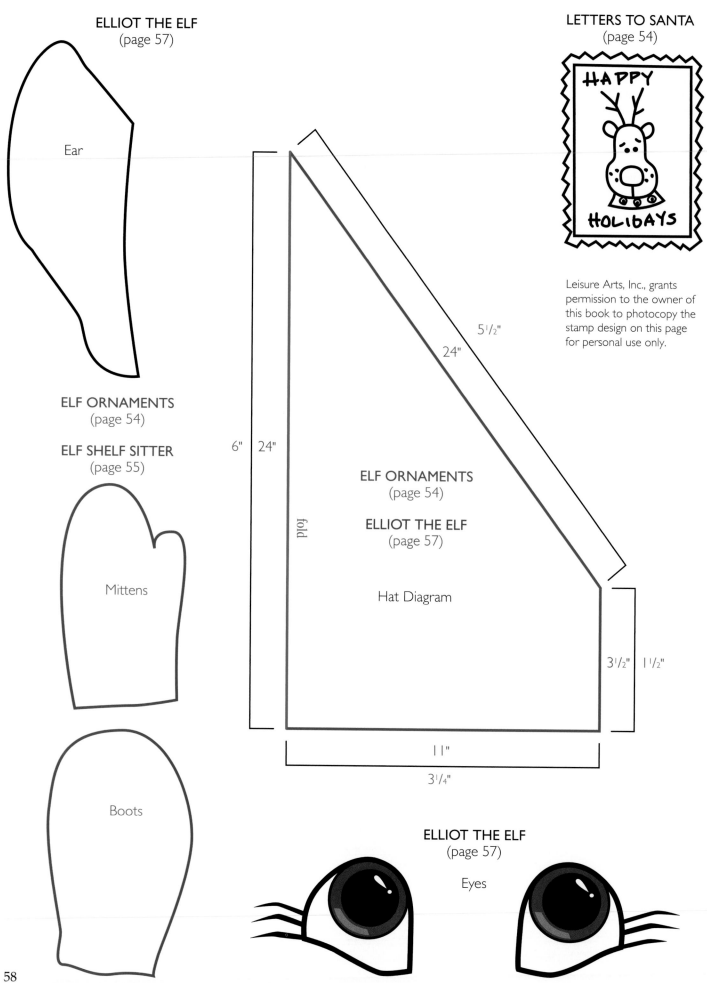

ELLIOT THE ELF
(page 57)

Ear

LETTERS TO SANTA
(page 54)

HAPPY

HOLIDAYS

ELF ORNAMENTS
(page 54)

ELF SHELF SITTER
(page 55)

Mittens

5¹/₂"

24"

6"   24"

fold

ELF ORNAMENTS
(page 54)

ELLIOT THE ELF
(page 57)

Hat Diagram

3¹/₂"   1¹/₂"

11"

3¹/₄"

Boots

ELLIOT THE ELF
(page 57)

Eyes

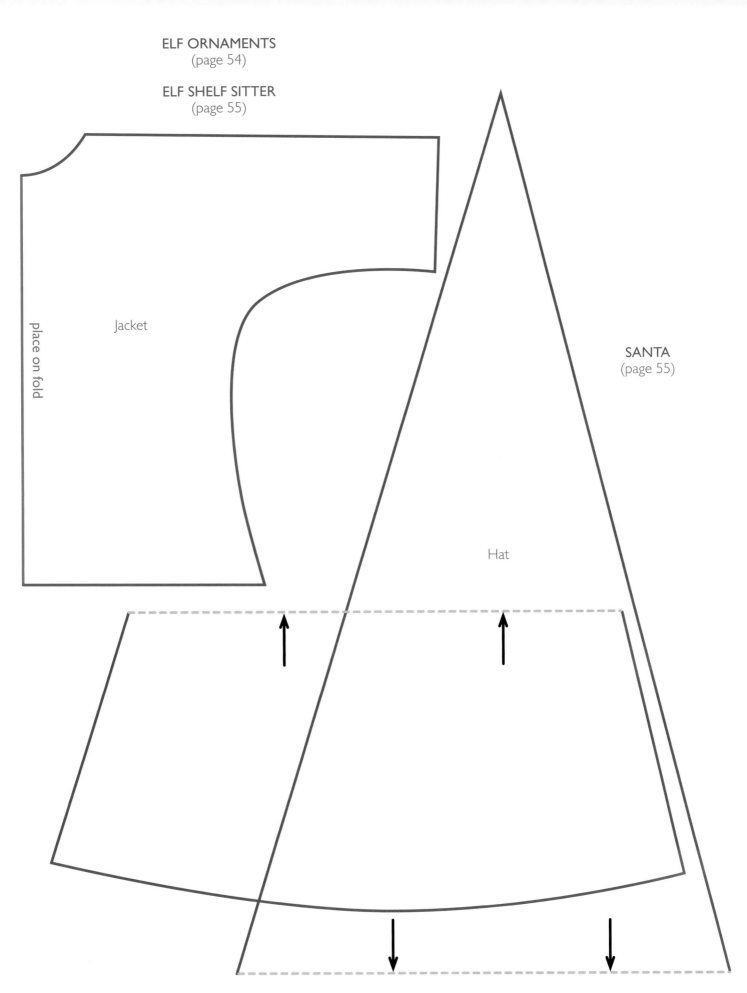

ELF ORNAMENTS
(page 54)

ELF SHELF SITTER
(page 55)

place on fold

Jacket

SANTA
(page 55)

Hat

A "BEAD-DAZZLED" CHRISTMAS

In the late 1800's, hobbyists delighted in making luxurious beaded items for their homes at very little expense. Now you can learn this beautiful craft, too! A touch of velvet and a pretty bead fringe is all it takes to turn this **Dazzling Lampshade** (page 68) into a glowing holiday accent! To make your own "Bead-Dazzled" Christmas, turn to page 66.

This "Bead-Dazzled" Christmas Tree (page 66) is ablaze with shimmering treasures! Little porcelain beauties, the sweet **Angel Ornaments** (page 66) wear gold ribbon gowns. Satiny glass adornments look truly luxurious when transformed into **Beribboned and Bedazzled Ornaments** (page 66). Eternal themes are embroidered on **Peace, Love, and Joy Pillow Ornaments** (page 68). Beaded **Tree Jewelry Ornaments** (page 67) add the rich look of cut crystal, while hand-dyed **Beaded Tassel Ornaments** (page 67) bring their own soft elegance to the branches. (Shown on page 61) Gold ruffles gather around a sumptuous **Victorian Velvet Tree Skirt** (page 67). For an easy accent, we scattered a handful of round golden beads among the velvet folds.

W rapped with swirling wire, these delicate **Beaded Candles** (page 68) are amazingly easy to create. They're perfectly complemented by red candles, faux berries, and greenery.

With a regal red robe and a beaded diadem for a halo, the **Elegant Angel Tree Topper** (page 68) is a heavenly messenger of good Christmas tidings. And little bead starbursts will spark the festivities when you hang up this Victorian **Velvet Stocking** (page 67). It's sure to gather both Christmas treats and compliments!

A "BEAD-DAZZLED" CHRISTMAS

*Draped with beaded **Tree Jewelry Ornaments**, this "Bead-Dazzled" Christmas Tree (shown on page 61) captures the romance of yesterday. A plush red **Victorian Velvet Tree Skirt** is richly edged with gold ruffles. Porcelain **Angel Ornaments** in golden dresses are quick to craft with their ready-made features. Ordinary glass adornments become treasures to cherish when transformed into **Beribboned and Bedazzled Ornaments**. The muted tones of **Beaded Tassel Ornaments** blend shades of scarlet with the purple sheen of the artificial grape clusters. Silk poinsettias, grape leaves, and hydrangeas are prettiest when nestled near beaded **Peace, Love, and Joy Pillow Ornaments**. And finally, with her scarlet and gold finery, the name of our **Elegant Angel Tree Topper** says it all.*

ANGEL ORNAMENTS
(Shown on page 62)

For each ornament, you will need a 4" square of muslin, polyester fiberfill, white pipe cleaner, hot glue gun, small porcelain doll hands and head, 9" and 14" lengths of 6"w gold organdy wired ribbon, 14" of 4"w pleated gold metallic wired ribbon, 1/4"w gold metallic ribbon, beading needle, gold metallic thread, iridescent and gold seed beads, 3 x 6mm clear oval beads, 5" of 26-gauge beading wire, and a pair of 5"h gold embroidered wings.

1. For body, fold muslin square in half. Using a 1/4" seam allowance, and leaving one short end open for stuffing, sew edges together to form tube; turn right side out. Stuff tube with fiberfill; work *Running Stitches*, page 158, along raw edge of opening; pull thread tightly to gather muslin; knot thread ends.
2. For arms, cut a 4 1/2" length from pipe cleaner; glue one hand at each end. Center and glue arms across shoulders under head; glue head to body.
3. For bodice, fold each end of 9" ribbon length 2" to wrong side; glue to secure. Fold ribbon in half lengthwise. Cut a slit in fold at center of ribbon long enough for head to fit through. Place bodice over head. Glue long edges together to form sleeves. Gathering slightly, spot glue bodice to body front and back.
4. For skirt, cut a 14" length each from 6"w and 4"w ribbon. Pulling end of wire along one edge of each 14"

ribbon, gather ribbon to fit around body. Fold ends of ribbon 1/4" to wrong side, bending wire ends to secure; trim excess wire. Overlapping ends and covering bottom edge of bodice, place 6"w, then 4"w gathered ribbons around body. Glue at back to secure.
5. With bow at back of skirt, tie 1/4"w ribbon around waist.
6. For beaded drop trim, thread beading needle with gold thread. Take a small stitch near bottom edge of top layer of skirt. Thread needle with one gold, one iridescent, one oval, one iridescent, and one gold bead. Run needle around last bead and back through other beads. Take another stitch in skirt. Repeat to sew a beaded drop at 1/2" intervals along edge of skirt. Sew one beaded drop to center of bodice.
7. For halo, leaving a 1" stem, form wire into a circle. Thread gold seed beads onto circle and twist wire end around stem to secure. Add beads to stem; bend wire end to secure. Glue stem to back of head.
8. Glue wings to back of angel.

BERIBBONED AND BEDAZZLED ORNAMENTS
(Shown on page 62)

For each ornament, you will need a 3" dia. red glass ball ornament, wire cutters, gold craft wire, and 1 1/2"w gold sheer wired ribbon.

For ornament with stars, you will also need Stick and Peel™ sheeting, gold foil paper, tracing paper, craft glue, gold seed beads, and gold bugle beads.

For ornament with diamonds, you will also need gold gimp trim, tracing paper, Stick and Peel™ sheeting, beading needle, and gold seed beads.

For ornament with beaded icicle, you will also need 20-gauge gold beading wire, needle nose pliers, assorted beads, and 26-gauge beading wire.

1. For ornament with stars, remove paper from one side of Stick and Peel. Smooth foil onto Stick and Peel. Trace star pattern, page 69, onto tracing paper; cut out. Draw around pattern on paper side of Stick and Peel four times; cut out. Remove paper backing. Arrange and apply stars on ornament. Arrange and glue seed and bugle beads on ornament in a snowflake design; allow to dry.
2. For ornament with diamonds, dividing ornament in four equal sections, glue trim to ornament; allow to dry.
3. Trace diamond pattern, page 69, onto tracing paper; cut out. Draw around pattern on paper side of Stick and Peel four times; cut out. For each diamond, remove paper backing and apply one diamond to one section of ornament. For bead outline, thread beads onto needle with enough beads to cover one edge of diamond. Carefully lay beads along edge of diamond; press beads in place with finger while removing needle. Repeat for remaining three edges of diamond. Pressing beads onto diamond shape with fingers, fill in diamond with beads.
4. For ornament with beaded icicle, cut a 15" length of gold wire. Use pliers to make a loop in wire to fit around neck of ornament; twist and curl wire end to secure. Thread

desired beads onto wire. Bend and twist bottom 1 1/2" of wire end into a swirl design. For small beaded drop, refer to Step 6 of Angel Ornaments, page 66, to thread three beads onto 26-gauge wire. Attach drop to spiral at bottom of icicle.

5. For each ornament, tie a 20" length of ribbon into a bow around hanger on ornament.

BEADED TASSEL ORNAMENTS
(Shown on page 62)

For each ornament, you will need red and purple fabric dye, ecru tassel, assorted beads, hot glue gun, gimp trim, and 1 1/2"w ribbon.

1. Follow manufacturer's directions to dye bottom of tassel purple and top of tassel red. Lightly rinse with water; hang to dry.
2. Slide beads onto strands of tassel as desired; spot glue to secure.
3. Trimming to fit, glue trim around top of tassel.
4. Tie a length of ribbon into a bow; glue bow at top of tassel.

VICTORIAN VELVET TREE SKIRT
(Shown on page 61)

You will need a 46" square of red velvet, fabric marking pen, thumbtack, string, 1 yd. of gold sheer fabric, 8mm gold beads, beading needle, and beading thread.

1. For skirt, using a 2" measurement for inside cutting line and a 22" measurement for outside cutting line, follow Cutting a Fabric Circle, page 156, to cut circle from velvet. For back opening, cut skirt from inner circle to outer edge. Fold back opening and inner circle edges 1/4" to wrong side; stitch to secure.
2. For ruffle, piecing as necessary, cut a 7"w strip 7 3/4 yds. long from gold fabric. Fold strip in half lengthwise.

Working through both layers of fabric, work Running Stitches, page 158, along long raw edges; gather strip to fit outer edge of skirt. Pin ruffle to right side of skirt along outer edge. Use a 1/4" seam allowance to sew ruffle to skirt. Remove pins. Finger press seam allowance to wrong side. Sew along edge of skirt close to ruffle seamline to secure seam allowance.
3. Use beading needle and thread to sew beads to skirt as desired.

VELVET STOCKING
(Shown on page 65)

You will need tracing paper, 7" x 30" piece of crushed red velvet, clear nylon thread, 6mm gold beads, 3mm x 6mm gold oval beads, 20" of 5"w gold sheer wired ribbon, 1 yd. of 1 1/2"w gold ribbon, sprig of red velveteen flowers with gold leaves, hot glue gun, and 10" of gold cording.

1. Matching arrows and dashed lines, trace stocking top and stocking bottom patterns, page 154, onto tracing paper; cut out. Matching right sides and short edges, fold velvet in half. Use pattern to cut stocking pieces from velvet. Using clear thread, arrange and stitch beads in snowflake designs on right side of one stocking piece (front) as desired.
2. Matching right sides and using a 1/4" seam allowance, stitch stocking pieces together. Fold top of stocking 1/2" to wrong side; stitch to secure. Turn stocking right side out.
3. Fold 5"w ribbon in half lengthwise. Pull wire along both sides of ribbon to gather ribbon to fit around top of stocking; twist wire ends together to secure. Stitch wired edges of ribbon to outside top of stocking.
4. Use 1 1/2"w ribbon and follow Making a Bow, page 157, to make a bow with two 2 1/2" loops, two 2" loops and two 9" streamers. Stitch bow at top of stocking front. Glue leaves and flowers at center of bow.
5. For hanger, knot ends of cording together. Stitch knot at top inside of stocking at heel seam.

TREE JEWELRY ORNAMENTS
(Shown on pages 61 and 62)

For each ornament, you will need 15mm clear berry beads, 6mm clear faceted beads, 6mm round red beads, 6mm clear frosted round beads, 6mm gold round beads, and 4mm gold round beads.

For beaded swag, you will also need No Stretch™ nylon beading string and 20mm clear diamond drop beads.

For beaded icicle, you will also need wire cutters, 20-gauge gold wire, and needle nose pliers.

1. For beaded swag, cut a length of string the desired length of swag plus 2". For swag end sequence, knot one end of string through one diamond drop bead; thread one 6mm gold, one red, and one 6mm clear faceted bead onto string. Thread beads onto string in the following order: 4mm gold, berry bead, 4mm gold, red, and 6mm clear faceted. Leaving enough length to work swag end sequence (in reverse) at opposite end, repeat sequence until desired length of swag is beaded.
2. For each beaded drop on swag, knot one end of a 5" length of string through one diamond drop bead; thread beads onto string in the following order: 4mm gold, red, clear faceted, 4mm gold, berry bead, 4mm gold, clear faceted, red, and 4mm gold bead onto string. Knot end of beaded drop to swag as desired.
3. For each icicle, use pliers to shape 2" of one end of a 12" length of wire into a swirl shape. Leaving two to three inches at remaining end of wire unbeaded, thread beads onto wire as desired. Use pliers to shape remaining end of wire into a swirl shape.

BEADED CANDLES
(Shown on page 63)

You will need 20-gauge gold wire, wire cutters, needle nose pliers, assorted candles, and beads in assorted shapes and sizes.

1. For each candle, leaving extra wire at one or both ends, wrap wire around candle as desired. Carefully slip wire off candle.
2. Thread beads onto wire as desired; if necessary, use pliers to insert a small piece of wire into last bead to secure in place. Use pliers to shape extra wire at end(s) into a swirl design. Place beaded wire on candle.

DAZZLING LAMPSHADE
(Shown on page 60)

You will need a scalloped lampshade, crushed velvet to cover lampshade, strand of 4mm gold beads, beading needle, beading thread, 3" eye pins, assorted beads (we used iridescent seed beads, 6mm gold washer beads, and iridescent red pony beads), 1/2"w gimp trim, and a hot glue gun.

1. Referring to *Covering a Lampshade*, page 156, use velvet to cover lampshade.
2. Using needle and thread to secure strand at points between scallops, attach strand of beads along bottom edge of lampshade.
3. For each beaded drop, thread beads onto pin. Bend end of each pin into a hook shape.
4. Spacing drops evenly around lampshade, attach drops to strand of beads.
5. Glue trim along top and bottom edges of lampshade.

PEACE, LOVE, AND JOY PILLOW ORNAMENTS
(Shown on pages 61 and 62)

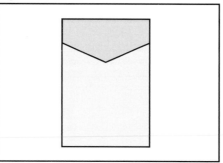

You will need tracing paper, plain and crushed velvet, tissue paper, beading needle, beading thread, gold seed beads, polyester fiberfill, iridescent seed beads, 4mm luster beads, and fabric glue.

1. For each pillow, trace flap pattern, page 69, onto tracing paper; cut out. Use pattern to cut flap from plain velvet. Cut an 5 1/2" x 8" piece of crushed velvet for pillow.
2. Glue edges adjacent to point on flap 1/4" to wrong side. Allow to dry.
3. Trace "Peace," "Love," or "Joy" pattern, page 69, onto tissue paper; cut out pattern 1/2" outside word. Pin pattern to center on right side of flap.
4. Thread beading needle with beading thread and sew beads to flap along lines of pattern; carefully remove tissue paper. To reinforce and straighten beads, come up with needle next to a bead at end of a line and run thread through all beads in a line. Take needle to wrong side of flap; knot thread end. For curved lines, repeat, going only through two or three beads at a time.
5. Referring to Fig. 1, match wrong side of flap on right side of pillow piece. Stitching close to edges, baste flap in place. With flap positioned between thicknesses and matching short ends, fold pillow piece in half. Using a 1/4" seam allowance and leaving an opening in one side of pillow for turning, sew edges together. Turn pillow right side out. Stuff pillow with fiberfill; sew opening closed.

Fig. 1

6. Take a small stitch along edge at one end of flap. Alternating gold and iridescent beads, thread seven seed beads, one luster bead, and seven seed beads onto needle. Take a small stitch on flap edge 3/4" from first stitch. Repeat to make three more scallops.
7. Using beading needle and thread, thread beads on needle for desired length of tassel. Run thread around last bead and back up through beads of strand. Take a small stitch on flap edge. Using desired beads, repeat to make two more strands.
8. Repeat Step 6 along remaining edge of flap. Knot and trim thread.

ELEGANT ANGEL TREE TOPPER
(Shown on page 64)

You will need a 4" square of muslin, polyester fiberfill, low-loft polyester batting, wire cutters, craft wire, white pipe cleaner, hot glue gun, porcelain hands and head, 2 1/2"w gold wired ribbon, red velvet, gold flat braid, fabric glue, 5"h gold embroidered wings, red seed beads, and 3 x 6mm gold oval beads.

Match right sides and use a 1/4" seam allowance for all sewing unless otherwise indicated.

1. Follow Steps 1 and 2 of Angel Ornament, page 66, to make body and attach head, arms, and hands.
2. For bodice, cut a 12" length from ribbon. Pulling wires at top and bottom, gather ribbon to measure 6". Overlapping ends at back, wrap ribbon around neck and body. Cut an opening at each side of bodice large enough for arms to fit through. Pull arms through openings; twist wire ends at back to secure.
3. For skirt, cut a 9" x 15" piece from velvet. Sew short edges together to form a tube. Fold remaining raw edges 1/4" to wrong side. Leaving a 4" tail at each end, work *Running Stitches*, page 158, along folded edges. Place skirt over body; pull thread ends to gather top of skirt just under bodice. Knot thread ends together to secure.

Stuff skirt with fiberfill until desired fullness is achieved. Pull thread ends tightly to gather bottom of skirt. Knot thread ends together to secure.

5. For sleeves, cut an 8¹/₂" × 10" piece from velvet. Matching long edges and leaving a 4" opening at center, stitch 3" along each end of long edges together to form a tube. Fold raw edges at center to wrong side; use fabric glue to secure; allow to dry. Fold raw edges at each end of tube ¹/₄" to wrong side. Stitch to secure. Use fabric glue to attach trim around ends of tube; allow to dry. Referring to Fig. 1, roll tube so that seam is facing front. Inserting through opening along long edges, insert arms through opening and out through ends of tube. Arrange sleeves around back and along arms of angel. Hot glue sleeves at wrists. Arrange arms as desired.

Fig. 1

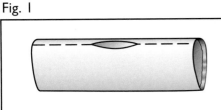

6. Cut wings apart at center. Use fabric glue to attach red beads to right side of each wing; allow to dry. Stitch wings at back of angel.
7. For halo, thread two seed beads, then one oval bead onto 3" of wire; repeat sequence until wire is covered. Twist ends of wire to secure. Hot glue halo to angel's head.

Beribboned and Bedazzled
Ornaments
(page 66)

Peace, Love, and Joy
Pillow Ornaments
(page 68)

Terrific Tablescapes

Christmas brings such a wonderful whirl of activities! And the best of these may be hosting fabulous meals in memorable settings. Whether the holidays find you planning a grand feast worthy of **Victorian Splendor** or organizing a more casual affair, we have the perfect decorating theme for the occasion. Turn to page 74 for project instructions and additional information on creating these fabulous "tablescapes."

Set among sweet-smelling candles and golden pillars, our **Celestial Celebration** (page 74) is the perfect decor for a formal buffet. The **Rise and Shine** (page 75) tablescape offers a casual yet festive way to greet the day. And if cozy is your cup of tea, then you'll love the warmth of the **Country Cabin** (page 75) setting with its rustic style!

VICTORIAN SPLENDOR TABLESCAPE

*Set your dining room for a glorious Christmas feast in Victorian style! Each chair boasts its own **Chairback Accent** tied with a golden bow. White linen table runners with Battenberg trim spread the length of the cranberry-draped table and across the sides at each place setting. The fabulous centerpiece begins with a six-foot length of artificial garland with its ends tucked to its center. The collection of ornaments nestled in the garland includes red satin glass balls, blown-glass candles, feather-tailed birds, and paper angels. Faux white roses and dogwood are tucked into the garland, adding to the vintage setting. On each plate, **Victorian "Crackers"** glow with Yuletide cheer beside little polished photo frames. The frames make ornate napkin holders, and they double as placecards when you add your guests' names.*

VICTORIAN "CRACKERS"

(Shown on pages 70 and 71)

For each cracker, you will need a 6½" x 10" piece of red fabric, toilet paper tube, hot glue gun, two 8" lengths of ⅛"w gold braid, small gift to fit in cracker, and 6½" of a 2½"w gold scalloped-edge paper border.

1. Overlapping long edges over tube, glue fabric around tube.
2. Knot one length of braid around fabric at one end of tube; trim ends close to knot. Place gift in tube. Knot remaining length of braid around fabric at opposite end of tube; trim ends.
3. Glue border around center of cracker.

CHAIRBACK ACCENT

(Shown on page 70)

For each accent, you will need an 18" long artificial pine branch, wire cutters, floral wire, 60" of ¼" dia. gold cord, gold-tipped artificial pine sprigs, artificial holly sprigs with berries, gold-tipped pinecones, silk rose, 30"

of 1½"w sheer gold wired ribbon, and a hot glue gun.

1. Arranging stems 5" from one end, wire pine, holly sprigs, pinecones, and rose to branch. Knot each end of cord. Leaving a 7" tail at each end and completely covering wires, wrap and glue cord around branch.
2. Tie ribbon into a bow around cord.
3. Tie ends of cord around chairback to attach accent to chair.

CELESTIAL CELEBRATION TABLESCAPE

*Heavenly desserts deserve stellar settings, and this delectable buffet will outshine all others this holiday season! At the base of the **Celestial Centerpiece** is an 18"-diameter wreath and two lengths of garland, both adorned with berry sprays, grape leaves, painted pinecones, glass ornaments, gold stars, and star garland. Golden serving plates resting on pillar candleholders offer up rich Christmas treats. A gilded stand adds elegance to a bottle of wine, and hurricane globes hold cream-colored candles. Beautifully protecting the surface are three **Tasseled Table Runners**.*

CELESTIAL CENTERPIECE

(Shown on page 72)

You will need a gold leaf kit; large candleholder for stand (our candleholder is 28"h with a 7" dia. tray); pinecones; assorted artificial leaves, artificial greenery and floral sprigs; artificial pine wreath to fit over candleholder (our wreath measures 18" dia.); wire cutters; floral wire; long floral picks; hot glue gun; glass ball ornaments; 6" dia. star ornament; utility knife; cutting mat; floral foam; 11" dia. acrylic plate; and artificial pine boughs.

1. For stand, follow manufacturer's instructions to apply gold leaf to candleholder; allow to dry. Place stand at center of table.
2. Arrange pinecones, leaves, greenery, sprigs, and ornaments on wreath; glue, wire, or use floral picks to secure in place. Place wreath over stand.
3. For centerpiece top, use utility knife

to cut pieces of floral foam to fit on plate. Glue foam pieces to plate.
4. Insert pine boughs into floral foam; glue as necessary to secure. Arrange pinecones, leaves, greenery, and sprigs between pine boughs; glue, wire, or use floral picks to secure in place. Wire ornaments to centerpiece as desired. Glue floral pick to star ornament; insert at top of centerpiece.
5. Glue centerpiece top to tray of stand.

TASSELED TABLE RUNNERS

(Shown on page 72)

For each table runner, you will need a fabric marking pen, 15½" x 60" gold fabric piece, ½"w paper-backed fusible web tape, metallic gold thread, two 3" long metallic gold tassels, and two 1³⁄₁₆" dia. gold shank buttons.

1. Matching long edges, fold table topper in half. Refer to Fig. 1, to cut a point at each short end of table topper.

Fig. 1

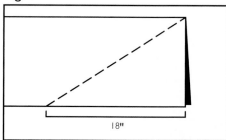

18"

2. Trimming to fit, fuse a length of web tape to wrong side of topper along each long edge; do not remove paper backing. Press each edge ½" to wrong side. Unfold edge, remove paper backing, and fuse in place. For each end, trimming to fit, fuse a length of web tape to wrong side of topper along edge of one side of point. do not remove paper backing. Press edge ½" to wrong side. Unfold edge, remove paper backing, and fuse in place. Repeat to fuse remaining edge of point on table runner.
3. Sew one tassel and one button to each point of table runner.

COUNTRY CABIN TABLESCAPE

Offering a warm yet rugged appeal, this rustic tablescape is simplicity itself! The **Country Tablecloth** *is a plaid fabric square with burlap and twig edgings.* **Twig Trees** *stand on a bark slab or on an overturned bark basket, while* **Grapevine Ball Candleholders** *stand in flowerpots. A purchased cabin forms a backdrop for resin figures of Mr. and Mrs. Claus. Even the purchased pottery dishes are rimmed in country red!*

COUNTRY TABLECLOTH
(Shown on page 73)

You will need fabric for tablecloth (our finished tablecloth measures 44" square), natural burlap for borders, fabric glue, 1" dia. and 1½" dia. grapevine stars, small evenly cut straight twigs, and a hot glue gun.

1. Cut a piece of fabric for desired size tablecloth; fray edges ⅛".
2. Cut 2"w strips of burlap to fit along edges of fabric piece; fray edges ¼". Overlapping ends of strips at corners, use fabric glue to glue strips ¾" from edges of tablecloth; allow to dry.
3. Hot glue one 1½" dia. star at each corner of border. Spacing evenly, and alternating stars and twigs, hot glue stars and twigs along borders.

GRAPEVINE BALL CANDLEHOLDERS
(Shown on page 73)

You will need a decorative flowerpot (we used a 3½" dia. x 5"h textured-painted pot), fabric, craft glue, natural burlap, a 4" dia. grapevine ball, pillar candle, utility scissors, artificial greenery with berries, hot glue gun, and a miniature redbird (optional).

1. Tear a strip from fabric to fit around rim of pot; use craft glue to glue fabric around rim. Allow to dry.
2. Measure around pot and add 15". Pull several threads from burlap. Trim

to determined measurement. Tie lengths into a bow around rim.
3. Using utility scissors to clip vines, clip a hole in one side of grapevine ball for bottom of candle to fit through.
4. With hole for candle at top, hot glue ball to pot. Insert candle in hole. Hot glue greenery and berries to ball. If desired, hot glue redbird to ball.

TWIG TREES
(Shown on page 73)

You will need twig trees, small holly berry garland, miniature redbirds, hot glue gun, flat-edged basket with bark sides, and bark pieces.

1. Drape twig trees with small holly berry garland. Place miniature redbirds in branches; glue to secure.
2. Turn basket upside down. Glue one tree to bottom of basket. Glue pieces of bark to bottom of basket around base of tree.

RISE AND SHINE TABLESCAPE

Encourage your holiday sleepyheads to rise and shine for a breakfast or brunch served from this splendid sideboard! Provide festive plates and flatware bundles dressed up with our **Napkin and Napkin Ring Sets** *featuring beads from tree garland. The menu tree is an artificial pine that's quick to decorate with bows, bead garland, and a papier-mâché star. You may wish to bend a few branch tips to secure the* **Chalkboard Menu** *to the tree.* **Star Topiaries** *fill in any empty spots, adding lively color and playfulness. And don't forget the easy-to-piece* **Patchwork Table Runner**. *Its pattern of small squares echoes the look of the checkerboard ribbon and the menu border.*

CHALKBOARD MENU
(Shown on page 73)

You will need masking tape; 8⅝" x 11⅝" framed chalkboard; white spray primer; four 1½"w wooden stars; white, yellow, red, and black acrylic paint; paintbrushes;

hot glue gun; four ½" dia. red buttons; and white chalk.

Allow primer, paint, and glue to dry after each application.

1. Leaving frame unmasked, use masking tape to mask chalkboard.
2. Apply primer to chalkboard frame and stars.
3. Paint top and inside edge of frame white. Use a pencil to lightly draw a checkerboard design on top of frame. Paint every other square on checkerboard black. Paint outside edge of frame red. Paint stars yellow.
4. Remove masking tape from chalkboard.
5. Glue buttons to stars; glue stars to corners of chalkboard.
6. Use chalk to write menu on chalkboard.

STAR TOPIARIES
(Shown on page 73)

For each topiary, you will need white spray primer; desired-size clay flowerpot; yellow, red, and green acrylic paint; paintbrushes; 1"w black-and-white checked ribbon; low-temperature glue gun; utility knife; cutting mat; floral foam; 6½"w papier-mâché puffy star ornament; utility scissors; ¼" dia. wooden dowel; wood-tone spray; 10" of 1½"w red wired ribbon; and green excelsior.

Allow primer, paint, and wood-tone spray to dry after each application.

1. Apply primer to inside rim and outside of flowerpot. Paint inside rim and outside of flowerpot desired color.
2. Measure around rim of flowerpot; add ½". Cut a length from 1"w ribbon the determined measurement. Glue ribbon around rim of flowerpot.

continued on page 140

THE SHARING OF CHRISTMAS

Make your Christmas giving truly memorable! Beautiful accents for the home, appealing fashions for folks of all ages, and fabulous wrappings are just a few of the creative offerings you'll find in this wonderful collection. Remember a dear friend with a lovely crocheted afghan or fancy beaded fringe handbag. Little ones will love a whimsical hand-painted sweatshirt, and your favorite man is sure to look festive in a unique vest. Or show off your handiwork with an exquisite wine bottle bag or embellished accent lamp. A handmade gift is truly from the heart, so share a little of yourself with the special people on your list.

Our **Beaded Lampshade** (page 90) is the ultimate in sophistication with black braid and iridescent bead fringe. It tops a bronze candlestick lamp in style!

For an elegant presentation, wrap a gift of spirits in this easy-to-make **Bedazzled Bottle Bag** (page 87) — so festive with sparkling beaded tassels!

Give a gift that's doubly warming! This **Cozy Crocheted Afghan** (page 87) will protect from drafts, and your thoughtfulness will warm the heart.

S ometimes the simplest materials make the grandest of gifts! Cover a denim three-ring binder with flannel patches and felt appliqués to create a wonderful **Patchwork Memory Album** (page 88). Send wishes for a snowy holiday with our **Wintry Wall Hanging** (page 88), and place your most special offerings in these soft **Flannel Gift Bags** (page 88).

Attention all Santas! Don't your favorite little elves deserve these **"I've Been Very Good" Sweatshirts** (page 90)? The cute designs are painted, appliquéd, and embellished with patches or bows. A few quick embroidery stitches add color to the neckline and cuffs.

Transform a simple thermal shell and jacket into a holiday-ready **Ladies' Twin Set** (page 89). The practical apparel comes to life when you add lace, ruched ribbon, appliquéd stars, and a caroling angel trio.

Here's a handsome accessory that's quick to make! This **Men's Faux Vest** (page 87) is created by adding buttons to a purchased muffler. It's a great gift for that special someone on your list.

Give her exciting jewels for her hair — handcrafted by you! These beaded hair pins will delight a fashion-conscious miss. Instructions for creating your own **Beaded Jewelry** are on page 91.

Whoever knew a gift of glamour could be so simple and inexpensive? This ring-bead necklace is just one beautiful example of how to create variety using novelty beads.

Let your imagination be your guide when making exotic accessories like this lapis lazuli-inspired necklace. The blue and gold colors are reminiscent of the semi-precious stone.

Jewelry making is an endlessly rewarding craft! For example, by using more rings in this bracelet, you can create an anklet or a fashionable matching choker.

Spread Christmas cheer with glistening jewelry inspired by beribboned sprigs of pine! You can use short lengths of wire or long pins to form the "pine needles."

85

*S*parkling bead fringe
adds style to this **Beaded
Handbag** (page 91).
*For even more evening
radiance, we sewed
tiny silver bead clusters
here and there on the
ready-made bag.*

A perfect match for our
handbag, this rich **Beaded
Blouse** (page 90) gleams
with elegance when you
sew on shining glass beads
in silver and teal.

COZY CROCHETED AFGHAN

(Shown on page 79)

Finished Size:
45" × 65½"

You will need 35 ounces, (990 grams, 1,775 yards) of brushed acrylic worsted weight yarn and size I (5.50 mm) crochet hook or size needed for gauge.

GAUGE: In pattern,
(ch 1, dc) 4 times = 3"; 5 rows = 3½"

Gauge Swatch: 3¾"w × 3½"h
(at tallest point)
Ch 14 **loosely.**
Work same as Afghan Body for 5 rows.
Finish off.

AFGHAN BODY
Ch 110 **loosely.**
Row 1 (Right side): Dc in sixth ch from hook, ★ ch 1, skip next ch, dc in next ch; repeat from ★ across: 53 dc and 53 sps.

Row 2: Ch 4 (counts as first dc plus ch 1, now and throughout), turn; ★ dc in next dc, 5 dc in next dc, ch 2, skip next dc, dc in next dc, ch 1; repeat from ★ across to last sp, skip next ch, dc in next ch: 93 dc.

Rows 3-84: Ch 4, turn; dc in next dc, ★ 5 dc in next dc, ch 2, skip next 4 dc, dc in next dc, ch 1, dc in next dc; repeat from ★ across.

Row 85: Ch 4, turn; (dc in next dc, ch 1) twice, skip next dc, sc in next dc, ch 1, ★ skip next 2 dc, (dc in next dc, ch 1) 3 times, skip next dc, sc in next dc, ch 1; repeat from ★ across to last 4 dc, skip next 2 dc, dc in next dc, ch 1, dc in last dc; do **not** finish off: 54 sts and 53 ch-1 sps.

EDGING
Rnd 1: Ch 1, do **not** turn; working in end of rows, 3 sc in first row, 2 sc in each of next 2 rows, (3 sc in next row, 2 sc in each of next 2 rows) across to last row, 5 sc in next corner

sp; working in sps across beginning ch, 2 sc in each of next 7 sps, 3 sc in next sp, (2 sc in each of next 5 sps, 3 sc in next sp) 6 times, 2 sc in each of next 7 sps, 5 sc in next corner sp; working in end of rows, 2 sc in each of next 2 rows, (3 sc in next row, 2 sc in each of next 2 rows) across to last row, 5 sc in next corner sp; working in sps across Row 85, 2 sc in each of next 7 ch-1 sps, 3 sc in next ch-1 sp, (2 sc in each of next 5 ch-1 sps, 3 sc in next ch-1 sp) 6 times, 2 sc in each of last 8 ch-1 sps; join with slip st to first sc: 624 sc.

Rnd 2: Ch 2, hdc in same st and in each sc around working 3 hdc in center sc of each corner 5-sc group, hdc in same st as first hdc; join with slip st to top of beginning ch-2: 632 sts.

Rnd 3: Ch 5 (counts as first dc plus ch 2), (dc, ch 2, dc) in same st, ch 3, skip next 3 hdc, dc in next hdc, ch 3, ★ † [skip next 5 hdc, dc in next hdc, (ch 2, dc) 3 times in same st, ch 3, skip next 5 hdc, dc in next hdc, ch 3] across to within 3 hdc of center hdc of next corner 3-hdc group, skip next 3 hdc †, dc in center hdc, (ch 2, dc) 3 times in same st, ch 3, skip next 3 hdc, dc in next hdc, ch 3; repeat from ★ 2 times **more**, then repeat from † to † once, dc in same st as first dc, ch 2; join with slip st to first dc: 54 4-dc groups.

Rnd 4: Ch 3, (2 dc, ch 2, 2 dc) in first ch-2 sp, dc in next dc, 2 dc in next ch-2 sp, dc in next dc, sc in next 2 ch-3 sps, dc in next dc, 2 dc in next ch-2 sp, ★ dc in next dc, (2 dc, ch 2, 2 dc) in next ch-2 sp, dc in next dc, 2 dc in next ch-2 sp, dc in next dc, sc in next 2 ch-3 sps, dc in next dc, 2 dc in next ch-2 sp; repeat from ★ around; join with slip st to top of beginning ch-3.

Rnd 5: Slip st in next dc, ch 1, sc in same st, ch 3, (sc, ch 5, sc) in next ch-2 sp, (ch 3, skip next dc, sc in next dc) 3 times, ★ skip next 2 sc, (sc in next dc, ch 3, skip next dc) 3 times, (sc, ch 5, sc) in next ch-2 sp, (ch 3, skip next dc, sc in next dc) 3 times; repeat from ★ around to last 6 sts,

skip next 2 sc, (sc in next dc, ch 3, skip next dc) twice; join with slip st to first sc, finish off.

MEN'S FAUX VEST

(Shown on page 83)

You will need a man's muffler (we used a 7⅜" × 56" wool muffler with fringed ends) **and three buttons.**

Refer to diagram to work buttonholes and sew buttons on muffler.

Diagram

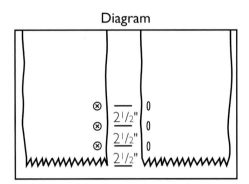

BEDAZZLED BOTTLE BAG

(Shown on page 78)

You will need an 18" square cloth napkin, 750ml gift bottle, rubber band, 18" of 1"w wired ribbon, two beaded tassels, and a hot glue gun.

1. For bag, match right sides and fold napkin in half. Leaving one short side open and sewing along inside edge of hem, sew edges of napkin together. Turn bag right side out.

2. Place bottle in bag. Gather bag around top of bottle; secure with rubber band. Fold ends of ribbon ½" to wrong side; glue in place. Wrap ribbon twice around top of bottle, covering rubber band; knot to secure. Thread streamer ends through tassel loops. Fold ends to wrong side; glue in place.

WINTRY WALL HANGING
(Shown on page 81)

You will need blue flannel; blue felt; red-and-black check flannel; white-and-black check flannel; black felt; ecru and black embroidery floss; tracing paper; gold, red, green, tan, brown, flesh, orange, and black felt pieces for appliqués; fabric glue; two 3" x 10" pieces of tissue paper; and a 16" long twig.

Refer to Embroidery Stitches, page 158, before beginning project. Use three strands of black floss for all stitches and work through all thicknesses unless otherwise indicated. Allow glue to dry after each application.

1. Cut an 11" x 14¹⁄₄" large background and four 1" x 4" hanging loops from blue felt, a 7" x 10¹⁄₂" small background from black felt, four 2¹⁄₂" corner squares and one ³⁄₄" x 2" hat band from white-and-black flannel, and three 4" square blocks from red-and-black flannel.
2. Press edges of each flannel square ¹⁄₄" to wrong side. Position one corner square at each corner of large background; work *Running Stitches* to secure to background. Center one heart at center of each corner square; work *Blanket Stitches* to secure to square.
3. Trace patterns, pages 91 and 92, onto tracing paper. Use patterns to cut four heart A appliqués; three each of tree and trunk appliqués; two ear muff appliqués; and one each of heart B, nose, pom-pom, mustache, beard, snowman, reindeer, muzzle, inner ear A, inner ear B, antler A, antler B, ear muff band, hat, star, and carrot nose appliqués from felt pieces. Rough cut six ¹⁄₈" - ¹⁄₄" squares for snowman eyes and mouth pieces from black felt.
4. Center small background on large background. Position blocks in a checkerboard design on small background, pin in place. Work *Running Stitches* along edges of blocks. Use ecru floss and work *Blanket Stitches* around black "blocks."

5. Overlapping as necessary, and using *Running Stitches* for snowman, reindeer, and Santa; *Blanket Stitches* for trees, reindeer muzzle, and ear muffs; *Straight Stitches* for carrot nose; *French Knots* for eyes on reindeer and Santa and for details on one tree and sides of background; and glue for remaining appliqués, arrange and attach appliqués to background.
6. Trace "Let it snow," page 147, twice onto separate pieces of tissue paper. Pin patterns along top and bottom of large background. Use ecru floss to work *Backstitches* over traced lines. Remove pins. Carefully remove tissue paper.
7. Cut a 14" x 17¹⁄₄" backing from blue flannel. Matching right sides and using ¹⁄₄"w seam allowance, sew one long and two short edges of backing together; turn right side out. Press open edges ¹⁄₄" to wrong side. Matching short ends, fold hanging loops half. Spacing loops evenly, pin ends of loops ¹⁄₂" inside opening. Topstitch ¹⁄₄" from each edge of backing. Remove pins.
8. Glue wall hanging to backing. Thread branch through loops.

PATCHWORK MEMORY ALBUM
(Shown on page 80)

You will need ecru, gold, red, blue, green, and brown felt; pinking shears; scraps of blue-and-black check, light plaid and dark plaid flannel; straight pins; gold, green, and black embroidery floss; tracing paper; tissue paper; and an 11³⁄₄" x 11³⁄₄" denim-covered scrapbook.

Refer to Embroidery Stitches, page 158, before beginning project. Use three strands of floss for all embroidery. Use black embroidery floss unless otherwise indicated.

1. Cut two 3" x 4" pieces from blue-and-black check flannel, two 2¹⁄₂" x 3¹⁄₂" pieces from blue felt, two 2" x 2¹⁄₄" pieces from red felt, one 2¹⁄₂" x 2³⁄₄" piece and one 3" x 3¹⁄₄" piece each from light plaid and dark

plaid flannel. Use pinking shears to cut a 9³⁄₄" x 10¹⁄₄" piece of ecru felt for background. Press edges of each flannel piece ¹⁄₄" to wrong side.
2. For border, refer to Diagram, this page, to pin felt and flannel pieces to background. Work *Blanket Stitches* along outer edge of border. Work *Running Stitches* along remaining edges of border pieces. Remove pins.
3. Trace tree, trunk, star, and heart B patterns, pages 91 and 92, onto tracing paper; cut out. Use patterns to cut four of each shape from felt. Overlapping as necessary, and using *Running Stitches* for tree trunks, *Blanket Stitches* for trees and hearts, and *Straight Stitches* and gold floss for details on stars, arrange and attach appliqués on border.
4. Trace "Holiday Memories," page 155, onto tissue paper. Pin tissue paper to center of background. Use *Backstitches* and *French Knots* to stitch over traced lines. Remove pins. Carefully remove tissue paper. Glue background to front of album.

Diagram

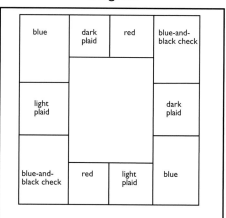

blue	dark plaid	red	blue-and-black check
light plaid			dark plaid
blue-and-black check	red	light plaid	blue

FLANNEL GIFT BAGS
(Shown on page 81)

For each bag, you will need a 10¹⁄₄" x 14¹⁄₂" piece of blue flannel; 5" square large background from gold or green felt; 4" square small background and ¹⁄₂" x 6³⁄₄" strip from light or dark plaid flannel; pinking shears; fabric glue; white, red, and black embroidery floss; and two ¹⁄₂" dia. buttons.

For Santa Bag, you will also need tracing paper; $3/4$" x 2" piece of black-and-white check flannel for hat brim appliqué, contrasting color of plaid flannel for hat, white and tan felt pieces for remaining appliqués.

For Reindeer Bag, you will also need tracing paper and red and brown felt pieces.

Refer to Embroidery Stitches, page 158, before beginning project. Use three strands of floss for all embroidery stitches. Work stitches through all thicknesses unless otherwise indicated.

1. Matching right sides and short edges, fold blue flannel piece in half. Using a $1/4$" seam allowance, sew sides of bag; turn right side out. Use pinking shears to trim top of bag. Measuring $1^{1}/_{2}$" from bottom of bag, center large then small background on bag front; spot glue to secure. Use red or black floss to work *Blanket Stitches* around large background and black or white floss to work *Running Stitches* around small background. Fold top of bag $1^{1}/_{2}$" to front. Glue plaid strip along center of flap; unfold flap. Sewing through single thickness only, sew one button at center of strip on flap and one button to center top of background square on front of bag.
2. For Santa bag, trace Santa face patterns, page 93, onto tracing paper. Use patterns to cut out shapes from felt pieces. Arrange and glue shapes to small background.
3. Use floss to work *French Knots* for eyes; *Running Stitches* around pompom, hat brim, beard, and mustache; and *Blanket Stitches* around hat.
4. For Reindeer bag, use reindeer face patterns, page 92, and refer to Step 2 to glue shapes to small background. Use floss to work French Knots for eyes; *Running Stitches* around antlers, inner ears, head, and nose; *Blanket Stitches* around muzzle; and a *Straight Stitch* for muzzle detail.
5. Knot one end of 10" length of floss around button on flap. Knot loose end of floss. Fold top edge of bag $1^{1}/_{4}$" to front. Place gift in bag. Close bag by wrapping floss around buttons.

LADIES' TWIN SET
(Shown on page 83)

You will need a tea bag; assorted cotton doilies; $3/8$"w and $1/2$"w flat cotton lace; lightweight ecru jacket and matching shell; tracing paper; gold, red, and green fabrics for appliqués; clear and gold glass seed beads; straight pins; assorted buttons; drawing compass; unbleached muslin; transfer paper; polyester fiberfill; ecru, gold, pink, green, and brown embroidery floss; three 2" dia. cotton doilies for angel dress collars; tissue paper; 1"w wired ribbon; assorted heart charms; and clear nylon thread.

Refer to Embroidery Stitches, page 158, before beginning project. Use three strands of floss for all embroidery stitching.

1. To tea dye doilies and lace, steep one tea bag in two cups hot water; allow to cool. Remove tea bag. Immerse doilies and lace in tea and soak until desired color is achieved; remove from tea, allow to dry, and press.
2. Measure around neck of shell; add 1". Cut a length of $1/2$"w lace the determined measurement. Overlapping ends at back, use nylon thread and a medium-width zigzag stitch to sew lace $1/2$" from edge of neck opening. Using green floss, work *Backstitches* along edge of opening. Sew buttons and charms along neckline.
3. Trace star pattern, page 148, onto tracing paper. Use pattern to cut three stars from green fabrics. Clip inner corners of stars and press edges $1/4$" to wrong side. Sew several clusters of three beads to stars. Leaving an opening for stuffing, arrange and blindstitch stars on jacket. Lightly stuff stars with fiberfill; blindstitch opening closed. Sew three or four buttons to center of each star.
4. For each angel, use compass to draw a 4" circle on muslin; cut out. Trace face pattern, page 148, onto tracing paper. Use transfer paper to

transfer face to center of one side (right side) of circle. Use floss to work *French Knots* for eyes, *Backstitches* for nose, and *Straight Stitches* for mouth and cheeks.
5. Turn raw edge of each circle $1/4$" to wrong side. Using a double strand of thread, work *Running Stitches* along turned edge. Pull ends of thread to gather circle. Lightly stuff circle with fiberfill; knot thread ends.
6. For each dress, cut a $2^{1}/_{2}$" x 7" piece of gold or red fabric. Press short ends $1/4$" to wrong side. Sew $3/8$"w lace to one long edge on right side. Baste along remaining long edge. Pull thread ends to gather edge tightly; knot ends to secure.
7. For each angel, pin one dress, one 2" dia. doily for collar, and one head to jacket. Stitch angel head to jacket through collar and gathered edge of dress. Stitch pressed edges of dress to jacket. Use gold floss to work *Straight Stitches* for halo. Sew several beads along halo.
8. For ribbon trim, measure around collar and down front of jacket. Cut a length of ribbon twice the determined measurement. Measure around hem of one sleeve. Cut two lengths of ribbon twice the determined measurement.
9. Beginning at left end of one ribbon length, mark top edge of each ribbon at 2" intervals. Beginning 1" from left end, mark bottom edge of ribbon at 2" intervals. Lightly mark a diagonal line between top and bottom edges where marked (Fig. 1). Using a double strand of matching thread, and knotting one end, work *Running Stitches* between marks on ribbon, pulling thread while stitching to gather ribbon to fit area to be trimmed.

Fig. 1

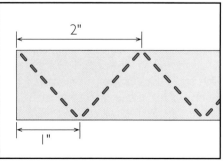

10. Pin ribbons to jacket. Use nylon thread to stitch in place; remove pins.
11. Sew charms and buttons to jacket as desired.

"I'VE BEEN VERY GOOD" SWEATSHIRTS
(Shown on page 82)

For each shirt, you will need a 6" square of muslin; tracing paper; transfer paper; white, cream, yellow, gold, flesh, pink, red, blue, green, brown, and dark brown acrylic paint; paintbrushes; black permanent fine-point marker; child's sweatshirt; scraps of fabric; sewing thread; paper-backed fusible web; two buttons (optional); and embroidery floss to contrast with sweatshirt.

Follow Painting Techniques, page 157, before beginning project. Allow paint to dry after each application.

1. Trace boy or girl pattern, pages 92 and 93, onto tracing paper. Use transfer paper to transfer design onto muslin. Paint design. Use marker to draw over outlines and detail lines.
2. To add binding around square, cut a 1½" x 26" strip from fabric and refer to Steps 5 - 11 of Patchwork Table Runner, page 140, to attach binding to front of square. Press binding outward. Fuse web to wrong side of square. Fuse square to sweatshirt. Topstitch along outer edges of binding.
3. Use six strands of contrasting floss to work *Running Stitches*, page 158, around neck and wrists of sweatshirt.
4. For boy's sweatshirt, trace elbow patch pattern, page 93, onto tracing paper; cut out. Use pattern to cut two elbow patches from fabric. Cut one 2¼" square and one 2" square patches from fabrics. Press edges of all patches ¼" to wrong side. Arrange and topstitch patches on sweatshirt.
5. For girl's sweatshirt, cut two ⅝" x 10" strips of fabric. Tie strips into bows. With one button over knot of each bow, sew bows and buttons at corners of binding.

BEADED LAMPSHADE
(Shown on page 78)

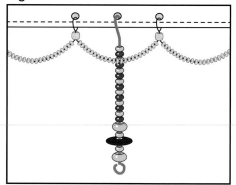

You will need 4¾"h x 5" dia. black lampshade; 1/16" dia. hole punch; thirty-two 2"l eye pins; 24-gauge jewelry wire; sixteen each of 6mm iridescent blue glass beads in round, roller, and wafer shapes; 32 small blue iridescent bugle beads; 272 gold frosted glass seed beads; 432 blue iridescent antique glass seed beads; 48 gold antique glass seed beads; 80 4mm gold glass beads; hot glue gun; black gimp trim; and a candlestick lamp base.

1. For beaded scallops, punch holes at ½" intervals along bottom edge of lampshade.
2. Leaving a 2" length of wire inside lampshade, refer to Fig. 1 and thread one pivot bead (bead used to end one scallop segment and begin another), 23 seed beads, then another pivot bead onto wire. Skip one hole in lampshade and thread wire through next hole and back through pivot bead. Continue to add 23 seed beads and pivot beads through every other hole to make scalloped trim. Twist wire ends together and work ends through beads.

Fig. 1

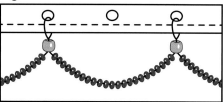

3. Leaving 1" unbeaded, refer to Fig. 2 to thread beads onto sixteen eye pins. Thread top of eye pins through remaining holes in lampshade. Use pliers to crimp tops of pins to secure.

Fig. 2

4. Leaving 1" unbeaded, refer to Fig. 3 to thread beads onto remaining eye pins. Thread tops of eye pins through loops in eye pins on lamp; use pliers to crimp tops of pins to secure.

Fig. 3

5. Trimming to fit, glue trim around top and bottom edges of lampshade.

BEADED BLOUSE
(Shown on page 86)

You will need a blouse with collar and cuffs, fine-point fabric marking pen, ruler, thread to match blouse, beading needle, small silver bugle beads, teal seed beads, silver seed beads, opalescent seed beads, and a ruler.

1. For bead fringe on collar and cuffs, use pen to lightly mark edge of collar and top edge of cuffs at ½" intervals.
2. Thread needle and knot one thread end. Coming up at first mark, thread one bugle bead, four teal beads, two opalescent beads, four teal beads, and one bugle bead onto needle. Take needle down at second mark.

3. Bring needle back up close to same mark and through last bugle bead. Thread four teal beads, two opalescent beads, four teal beads, and one bugle bead. Take needle down at next mark.

4. Repeat Step 3 until fringe is desired length. To finish, knot remaining end of thread on wrong side of blouse.

5. For bead outline on collar, cuffs, and front opening edges, use pen to lightly mark edges at $^{1}/_{4}$" intervals. Bring needle up at each mark, thread one silver bead onto needle and go back down near same mark. Come up at next mark and continue to add one bead at each mark. To finish, knot remaining end of thread on wrong side of blouse.

BEADED HANDBAG
(Shown on page 86)

 You will need a purchased crocheted handbag; a fine-point fabric marking pen; ruler; beading needle; thread to match handbag; small silver bugle beads; and teal, silver, and opalescent seed beads.

1. For bead fringe on top and bottom edges of handbag, use pen to lightly mark edges at $^{1}/_{2}$" intervals.

2. Thread needle and knot one thread end. Follow Step 2 and Step 3 of Beaded Blouse, page 90, until bead fringe is desired length. Knot remaining end of thread on inside of handbag.

3. For each bead cluster on side of handbag, use pen to lightly mark bag at 1" intervals. Thread needle and knot one thread end. Bring needle up, thread three silver beads onto needle, take needle back down in same hole and knot remaining end of thread to secure.

BEADED JEWELRY
(Shown on pages 84 and 85)

 Delight someone on your holiday gift list with jewelry made just for her! These gleaming necklaces and hair pins are one-of-a-kind works of art. Express your artistic side this

Christmas and create your own exciting jewelry designs.

Jewelry-making supplies are available from most retail craft stores and include a wide variety of products. We used seed beads, bugle beads, glass rings, and round beads to create our jewelry. For a professional-looking finish, be sure to match the color of clasps, head pins, and chains or any other hardware for each jewelry piece.

Lengthen or shorten chains by using needle-nose pliers to open and close the links. You may find links easier to handle by using tweezers to hold them while working. To reduce the likelihood of scratching links or other jewelry components, special solutions are available for coating the ends of your jewelry-making tools.

The necklace with large links is actually individual jump rings looped together and finished with a lobster clasp. We threaded a single bead onto each ring.

Holiday colors make the pine needle and red bow necklace bright. Short lengths of wire form the "needles," but long head pins cut to varying lengths would work just as well. The bow is a long piece of wire secured to the necklace and threaded with red seed beads before it is shaped.

Head pins hold the beads that dangle from one blue and gold necklace, while the remaining necklace uses a piece of leftover chain to attach a blue glass ring.

Bobby pins and silver-colored 24-gauge jewelry wire are the basis for the elegant hair ornaments.

To make your own beaded hairpin, make a tiny loop in one end of a long piece of wire. Thread the free end of the wire through the pin and then the loop. Tighten wire on pin by wrapping wire through pin a few times (Fig. 1).

Fig. 1

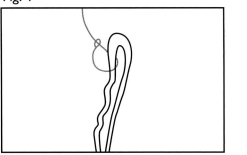

Now thread beads onto the wire, wrapping wire around pin occasionally as you shape your unique hairpin design. Keep the wire tight so your design will hold its shape.

To finish your hairpin, form a loop in the wire and wrap the wire through the loop and around the pin. Or try a decorative wire swirl for an added touch of elegance. To make a swirl, cut off beaded wire leaving a 3" to 5" wire end. Wrap the wire once around pin or beaded wire. Form a small loop in wire end. Holding the loop with pliers or tweezers, wrap the wire around the tool, making gradually larger circles.

Once you get started making your own jewelry, you'll be hooked! Try a variety of bead styles and colors. Some additional jewelry crafting ideas are pins, earrings, bracelets, and button covers. There is no end to the bejeweled gift possibilities!

WINTRY WALL HANGING
(page 88)

PATCHWORK MEMORY ALBUM
(page 88)

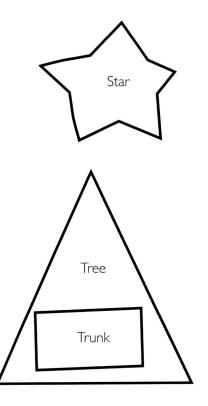

Star

Tree

Trunk

WINTRY WALL HANGING
(page 88)

FLANNEL GIFT BAGS
(page 88)

Antler A   Antler B

Reindeer

Inner Ear A   Inner Ear B

Nose

Muzzle

Ear Muff Band

Snowman

Ear Muff   Ear Muff

Carrot Nose

"I'VE BEEN VERY GOOD" SWEATSHIRTS
(page 90)

WINTRY WALL
HANGING
(page 88)

PATCHWORK
MEMORY ALBUM
(page 88)

Heart A

Heart B

I've been very Good

Pom-pom

Hat

Hat Band

Santa

Mustache

Beard

Elbow Patch

I've been Very Good

THE TASTES OF CHRISTMAS

Tempt the taste buds
of one and all with
selections from our
delectable array of
yummy Yuletide foods!
We've gathered recipes for
every occasion, from a casual
family breakfast or a "soup-er"
open house to a formal multi-course
meal, so planning your celebrations is
a breeze. You'll also find a collection
of dreamy desserts, as well as
scrumptious treats just perfect
for gift-giving. With every nibble
and sip of these irresistible treats,
you'll feel the magical spirit of the
most special season of the year!

Tamale Dressing, Herb Turkey Rub, Spicy Ginger-Cranberry Sauce

"Timeless" Traditions

Preparing traditional holiday foods is a labor of love, but being busy in the kitchen can mean missing fun with friends and family. With these step-saving recipes, you'll find fast and easy ways to make delicious dishes that are great for dinners and potlucks. Try the Green Beans Alfredo or the Nutty Sweet Potatoes for rave reviews. The Coffee Eggnog is a crowd-pleaser, too. You'll be surprised how quickly you can join in the merriment and the memory-making — without skimping on the flavors of Christmas!

TAMALE DRESSING

This Southwestern-style dressing goes great with smoked turkey.

- 2 cans (28 ounces each) tamales
- 2 boxes (6 ounces each) corn bread stuffing mix with seasoning packets
- 1 can (15¼ ounces) whole kernel corn, drained
- 1 can (15 ounces) black beans, drained
- 1 can (14½ ounces) chicken broth
- 1½ cups hot water
- 1 can (10 ounces) enchilada sauce
- 2 eggs, beaten

Preheat oven to 350 degrees. Reserving liquid from tamales, crumble tamales in a very large bowl. Add stuffing mix including seasoning from packets, corn, black beans, chicken broth, hot water, enchilada sauce, eggs, and reserved tamale liquid. Stir gently until well blended. Spoon dressing into a greased 9 × 13-inch baking dish. Cover with aluminum foil and bake 25 minutes. Uncover and bake 35 to 40 minutes or until top is golden brown. Serve warm.
Yield: about 15 servings

SPICY GINGER-CRANBERRY SAUCE

- 1 clove garlic, minced
- 1 tablespoon vegetable oil
- 2 cans (16 ounces each) whole cranberry sauce
- 1 tablespoon chopped crystallized ginger
- ⅛ teaspoon ground red pepper

In a medium saucepan, sauté garlic in oil over medium heat until softened. Stir in cranberry sauce, ginger, and red pepper. Stirring occasionally, cook about 7 minutes or until heated through. Store in an airtight container in refrigerator overnight to let flavors blend. Serve at room temperature.
Yield: about 3½ cups sauce

HERB TURKEY RUB

- ¼ cup dried rosemary leaves
- ¼ cup dried sage leaves
- 2 tablespoons garlic salt
- 1 tablespoon cracked black pepper
- 1 teaspoon dried thyme leaves

In a small bowl, combine rosemary, sage, garlic salt, pepper, and thyme; stir until well blended. Rub turkey with olive oil and herb rub before baking. Store any remaining rub in an airtight container.
Yield: about ½ cup dry rub

GREEN BEANS ALFREDO

- 3 cans (14¹/₂ ounces each) green beans, drained
- 1 jar (12¹/₂ ounces) boiled white onions, drained
- 2 jars (4¹/₂ ounces each) sliced mushrooms, drained
- 2 envelopes (1¹/₄ ounces each) Alfredo sauce mix and ingredients to prepare sauce
- ¹/₂ teaspoon salt
- ¹/₄ teaspoon ground black pepper
- ¹/₂ cup freshly grated Parmesan cheese

Preheat oven to 350 degrees. In a large bowl, combine green beans, onions, and mushrooms. Pour into a lightly greased 9 x 13-inch baking dish. Prepare Alfredo sauce mix according to package directions. Stir in salt and pepper. Pour sauce over green beans. Sprinkle cheese on top. Bake 30 to 40 minutes or until heated through and cheese is lightly browned. Serve warm.
Yield: about 12 servings

NUTTY SWEET POTATOES

- 2 cans (29 ounces each) sweet potatoes, drained
- 2 tablespoons butter or margarine, melted
- ¹/₄ teaspoon salt
- 2 jars (5 ounces each) pecans in syrup ice-cream topping

Preheat oven to 350 degrees. Place sweet potatoes in a 2-quart baking dish. Drizzle butter over potatoes and sprinkle with salt. Spoon topping over potatoes. Bake 30 to 40 minutes or until bubbly and heated through. Serve warm.
Yield: about 9 servings

Green Beans Alfredo, Nutty Sweet Potatoes

Easy Cheesy Bread, Brandied Fruit Sauce

EASY CHEESY BREAD

For an appetizer, use small French loaves.

- 1 loaf (16 ounces) unsliced French bread
- 1 1/2 cups combined shredded Monterey Jack and Colby cheese
- 3/4 cup butter or margarine, softened
- 2 tablespoons parsley flakes
- 1/2 teaspoon garlic powder
- 1/4 teaspoon onion powder
- 1/8 teaspoon ground red pepper

Cut 1-inch diagonal slices in bread without cutting through bottom of loaf. Transfer loaf to a large sheet of aluminum foil. In a medium bowl, combine cheese, butter, parsley, garlic powder, onion powder, and red pepper; stir until well blended. Spread 1 cup mixture between slices of bread and remaining mixture on top of loaf. Wrap foil over loaf without pressing top of bread. Loaf may be refrigerated until ready to bake.

Preheat oven to 425 degrees. Bake covered loaf 20 minutes. Uncover top of bread and bake 5 minutes or until cheese is lightly browned. Serve warm.

Yield: about 16 servings

BRANDIED FRUIT SAUCE

Dried fruit can be easily cut into pieces with kitchen shears.

- 2 packages (8 ounces each) mixed dried fruit, coarsely chopped
- 4 cups apple juice
- 1/4 cup sugar
- 1/2 cup brandy
- 1/2 teaspoon apple pie spice

In a medium saucepan, combine fruit, juice, and sugar. Stirring occasionally, cook over medium-high heat until mixture comes to a boil. Reduce heat to medium low and simmer about 30 minutes or until fruit is tender, stirring occasionally. Remove from heat; add brandy and apple pie spice. Serve warm with ham.

Yield: about 5 1/2 cups sauce

Lemon Fruitcake, Coffee Eggnog

LEMON FRUITCAKE

- 1 package (18 1/4 ounces) lemon cake mix
- 1/2 cup sweetened condensed milk
- 1/3 cup vegetable oil
- 1/4 cup water
- 2 eggs
- 1 1/2 cups golden raisins
- 1 1/2 cups chopped pecans

Preheat oven to 325 degrees. In a large bowl, beat cake mix, sweetened condensed milk, oil, water, and eggs at low speed of an electric mixer until moistened; beat at high speed 2 minutes. Stir in raisins and pecans. Spoon batter into 3 greased and floured 3 3/4 x 7 1/2-inch loaf pans. Bake 50 to 60 minutes or until a toothpick inserted in center of cake comes out with a few crumbs attached. Cool in pans 10 minutes. Remove from pans and cool completely on a wire rack. Store in an airtight container.

Yield: 3 loaves fruitcake

COFFEE EGGNOG

When serving in a punch bowl, soften ice cream and stir into eggnog.

- 1 can (1 quart) prepared eggnog, chilled
- 2 tablespoons instant coffee granules
- 1 pint coffee ice cream
- 1 tablespoon chocolate sprinkles to garnish

In a 1 1/2-quart pitcher, combine eggnog and coffee granules; stir until well blended. Place a small scoop of ice cream in each serving cup. Pour eggnog over ice cream. Garnish with chocolate sprinkles. Serve immediately.

Yield: about 6 cups eggnog

Burgundy Beef Stew, Dill and Green Onion Bread

"Soup-sational" Open House

Cold December nights and steaming, savory soups make perfect partners for casual get-togethers. Whether served with home-baked Dill and Green Onion Bread or buttery Seasoned Croutons, this soothing winter fare will have guests begging for more. And just when they think dinner couldn't get any better, serve a fresh-from-the-oven dessert and enjoy a chorus of heartfelt praise!

BURGUNDY BEEF STEW

- 3 pounds boneless beef chuck, cut into 1¹/₂-inch pieces
- ¹/₄ cup vegetable oil
- ¹/₃ cup all-purpose flour
- 2¹/₂ cups red Burgundy wine
- 2¹/₂ cups beef broth
- ¹/₄ cup tomato paste
- ³/₄ cup finely chopped celery
- 5 cloves garlic, minced
- 4 bay leaves
- 3 teaspoons chopped fresh thyme leaves, divided
- 1¹/₄ teaspoons salt
- ³/₄ teaspoon ground black pepper
- 1 pound small potatoes, cut in half
- 1 pound baby carrots
- 1 pound rutabagas, cut into 1-inch pieces
- 1 pound small onions
- 1 package (8 ounces) fresh mushrooms, cut in half
- ¹/₄ cup chopped fresh parsley

In an 8-quart Dutch oven, brown small amounts of meat at a time in oil over medium-high heat; set browned meat aside. Reduce heat to medium. Add flour to meat drippings; whisk constantly one minute or until lightly browned. Whisk in wine, beef broth, and tomato paste. Whisking frequently, bring mixture to a boil. Reduce heat to low. Add celery, garlic, bay leaves, 2 teaspoons thyme, salt, pepper, and meat. Cover and simmer 1³/₄ hours or until meat is tender. Add potatoes, carrots, rutabagas, and onions. Bring to a simmer; cover and cook about 45 minutes or until vegetables are tender. Add mushrooms and remaining 1 teaspoon thyme; simmer uncovered 10 minutes. Remove bay leaves. Stir in parsley. Serve hot.

Yield: about 16 cups stew

DILL AND GREEN ONION BREAD

- 1 package dry yeast
- 1 cup warm milk
- ¹/₄ cup butter or margarine, softened
- ¹/₄ cup sugar
- 1 egg
- 2 tablespoons finely chopped fresh dill weed
- 2 tablespoons finely chopped green onions
- 1 teaspoon salt
- 3³/₄ to 4 cups all-purpose flour
  Vegetable oil cooking spray
- 1 egg
- 1 tablespoon water
  Fresh dill sprigs and pieces of green onion blades to decorate

In a small bowl, dissolve yeast in warm milk. In a large bowl, combine butter, sugar, 1 egg, chopped dill weed, chopped onions, salt, and yeast mixture; beat until blended. Add 3³/₄ cups flour; stir until a soft dough forms. Turn onto a lightly floured surface and knead about 5 minutes or until dough becomes smooth and elastic, using additional flour as necessary. Place in a large bowl sprayed with cooking spray, turning once to coat top of dough. Cover and let rise in a warm place (80 to 85 degrees) one hour or until doubled in size.

Turn dough onto a lightly floured surface and punch down. Divide dough into fourths. Shape into two 4¹/₂-inch round loaves and two 12-inch-long baguette loaves. Place on 2 greased baking sheets. Spray tops of dough with cooking spray, cover, and let rise in a warm place one hour or until doubled in size.

Preheat oven to 350 degrees. In a small bowl, beat remaining egg and water; brush over loaves. Decorate with dill sprigs and green onion blades. Brush decorations with egg mixture. Bake 20 to 25 minutes or until bread is golden brown and sounds hollow when tapped. Serve warm or transfer to a wire rack to cool completely. Store in an airtight container.

Yield: 4 loaves bread

SWISS CHEESE CHOWDER

- 1¼ cups chopped onions
- ¾ cup chopped celery
- ¾ cup shredded carrots
- 2 cloves garlic, minced
- 6 tablespoons butter or margarine
- 6 tablespoons all-purpose flour
- 3 cans (14½ ounces each) chicken broth
- 3 cups diced potatoes
- ½ teaspoon salt
- ¼ teaspoon dry mustard
- ¼ teaspoon ground black pepper
- 1½ cups half and half
- 12 ounces bacon, cooked, crumbled, and divided
- 3 cups (12 ounces) finely shredded Swiss cheese
- 3 tablespoons chopped fresh parsley
  Crusty Bread Bowls to serve
  Parsley leaves to garnish

In a Dutch oven, sauté onions, celery, carrots, and garlic in butter over medium heat until vegetables are tender. Sprinkle flour over vegetable mixture; stir until flour begins to brown. Stirring constantly, gradually add chicken broth. Add potatoes, salt, dry mustard, and pepper. Increase heat to medium high; bring to a boil. Reduce heat to low; cover and cook about 10 minutes or until potatoes are tender. Stir in half and half. Reserving ½ cup bacon for garnish, stir in remaining bacon, cheese, and parsley; cook just until cheese melts.

To serve, spoon into Crusty Bread Bowls. Garnish with parsley leaves and reserved bacon; serve hot.

Yield: about 10 cups soup

CRUSTY BREAD BOWLS

- 2 packages dry yeast
- 2½ cups warm water
- 2 tablespoons vegetable oil
- 2 tablespoons sugar
- 2 teaspoons salt
- 5½ to 6½ cups all-purpose flour, divided
  Vegetable oil cooking spray
- 1 tablespoon yellow cornmeal
- 1 egg
- 1 tablespoon water

Swiss Cheese Chowder, Crusty Bread Bowl

In a large bowl, dissolve yeast in 2½ cups warm water. Stir in oil, sugar, and salt. Add 3 cups flour; beat with an electric mixer until blended. With a wooden spoon, stir in 2½ cups flour. Turn dough onto a lightly floured surface. Knead about 5 minutes or until dough becomes smooth and elastic, using additional flour as necessary. Place in a large bowl sprayed with cooking spray, turning once to coat top of dough. Cover and let rise in a warm place (80 to 85 degrees) one hour or until doubled in size.

Turn dough onto a lightly floured surface and punch down. Divide dough into 8 equal pieces. Shape each piece into a 3½-inch-diameter round loaf. Place loaves on 2 lightly greased baking sheets sprinkled with cornmeal. Spray tops of dough with cooking spray, cover, and let rise in a warm place 30 to 45 minutes or until doubled in size.

Preheat oven to 400 degrees. In a small bowl, beat egg and 1 tablespoon water. Brush tops of dough with egg mixture. Bake 15 to 20 minutes or until bread is golden brown and sounds hollow when tapped. Cover with aluminum foil if bread browns too quickly. Cool on a wire rack.

To serve, cut a ½-inch-thick slice from top of each loaf; hollow out center, leaving ½-inch-thick shell. Fill bread bowls with hot soup and serve with bread lids.

Yield: 8 bread bowls

ORANGE-RYE TOASTS

1   loaf (16 ounces) sliced
      rye cocktail bread
1/3 cup butter, softened
1/2 teaspoon orange extract

Place slices of rye bread in a single
layer on baking sheets. In a small
bowl, combine butter and orange
extract; stir until well blended. Spread
about 1/4 teaspoon butter on top side
of each slice of bread. Toast under
broiler. Serve with Beet Bisque.
Yield: about 3 1/2 dozen slices bread

BEET BISQUE

This recipe can be easily doubled.

1   cup chopped potato
1/2 cup chopped onion
1   tablespoon vegetable oil
1 1/2 tablespoons all-purpose flour
1   can (14 1/2 ounces) chicken
      broth
1   tablespoon chopped fresh
      tarragon leaves
3/4 teaspoon salt
1/4 teaspoon ground black pepper
1   can (15 ounces) sliced beets,
      undrained
     Fresh tarragon leaves to
      garnish

In a large saucepan, cook potato
and onion in oil over medium heat
until onion is tender, stirring
constantly. Stir in flour. Gradually stir
in chicken broth. Stir in 1 tablespoon
chopped tarragon, salt, and pepper.
Increase heat to medium high. Stirring
occasionally, bring to a boil. Reduce
heat to low; cover and simmer about
20 minutes or until potatoes are very
tender. Stir in beets. Process soup in
batches in a food processor until
smooth. Return soup to saucepan.
Cook until heated through. Garnish
with tarragon leaves and serve hot.
Yield: about 4 cups soup

Orange-Rye Toasts, Beet Bisque

CHICKEN GUMBO

- 1 chicken (about 4 pounds)
- 2 carrots, quartered
- 1 onion, quartered
- 2 ribs celery with leaves, cut into pieces
- 1 bay leaf
- 3 1/4 teaspoons salt, divided
- 2 teaspoons ground black pepper, divided
- 12 cups water
- 3/4 cup all-purpose flour
- 1/2 cup vegetable oil
- 2 cups chopped onions
- 2 cups chopped celery
- 1 cup chopped green pepper
- 4 cloves garlic, minced
- 1 package (16 ounces) frozen sliced okra
- 1 can (14 1/2 ounces) diced tomatoes, undrained
- 2 bay leaves
- 1 teaspoon dried thyme leaves
- 1/2 teaspoon ground red pepper
- 1 pound fresh shrimp, cooked, peeled, and deveined
- 1/4 cup chopped fresh parsley
- 1 1/2 tablespoons gumbo filé powder
  Hot pepper sauce to taste
  Hot cooked rice to serve

In an 8-quart stockpot, combine chicken, carrots, onion quarters, celery pieces, bay leaf, 2 teaspoons salt, and 1 teaspoon black pepper. Add water. Bring to a boil over high heat. Reduce heat to medium low; cover and simmer about one hour or until chicken is tender.

Strain and reserve broth; discard vegetables. Remove meat from chicken and cut into bite-size pieces; set aside. Stirring constantly, cook flour in hot oil in a large Dutch oven over medium heat 10 minutes or until mixture forms a brown roux. Reduce heat to medium low. Stir in chopped onions, 2 cups celery, green pepper, and garlic. Cook 15 minutes or until vegetables are tender. Stirring constantly, gradually add 6 cups reserved chicken broth. Stir in chicken, okra, tomatoes, bay leaves, thyme, remaining 1 1/4 teaspoons salt, remaining 1 teaspoon black pepper, and red pepper. Increase heat and bring to a boil. Reduce heat to low; cover and simmer 45 minutes. Stir in shrimp and parsley; cook about 3 minutes or until shrimp are heated through. Stir in filé powder and pepper sauce. Serve hot over rice.
Yield: about 14 1/2 cups gumbo

Chicken Gumbo

Fresh Cream of Tomato Soup, Seasoned Croutons

FRESH CREAM OF TOMATO SOUP

3 cups peeled, seeded, and
      chopped Roma tomatoes
      (about 1 1/4 pounds)
2 cups tomato juice
1/2 cup chopped onion
1/2 cup chopped celery
1/4 cup chopped fresh basil leaves
1 clove garlic, minced
1 teaspoon sugar
1 teaspoon celery salt
1/4 to 1/2 teaspoon salt
1/8 teaspoon ground red pepper
1 cup whipping cream
      Chopped fresh basil to garnish

In a large saucepan, combine
tomatoes, tomato juice, onion, celery,
basil, garlic, sugar, celery salt, salt, and
red pepper. Stirring occasionally, bring
to a boil over medium-high heat.
Reduce heat to low; cover and
simmer about 30 minutes or until
vegetables are tender. In a food
processor or blender, process soup in
batches until smooth. Return soup to
saucepan. Stirring constantly over low
heat, gradually add whipping cream.
Cook until heated through. Garnish
with basil leaves and serve hot.
Yield: about 5 cups soup

SEASONED CROUTONS

*An electric knife is useful for cutting the
bread into cubes.*

1 loaf (16 ounces) unsliced
      French bread

1/2 cup butter or margarine
1/2 teaspoon celery salt
1/2 teaspoon garlic powder
1/8 teaspoon ground red pepper

Preheat oven to 375 degrees.
Cut bread into 3/4-inch cubes (about
16 cups). Place in a large aluminum
roasting pan. In a small saucepan,
combine butter, celery salt, garlic
powder, and red pepper. Cook over
medium-low heat until butter melts.
Drizzle melted butter mixture over
bread cubes, tossing until evenly
coated. Bake 20 minutes, stirring
every 5 minutes or until golden
brown. Cool in pan. Store in an
airtight container. Serve with Fresh
Cream of Tomato Soup.
Yield: about 12 cups croutons

CHEDDAR CASSEROLE BREAD

1 package dry yeast
1/4 cup warm water
1/2 cup warm milk
1/3 cup butter or margarine, melted
1 egg
2 tablespoons sugar
1/2 teaspoon salt
1/4 teaspoon ground black pepper
1 cup (4 ounces) shredded sharp Cheddar cheese
1 cup all-purpose flour
1 cup whole-wheat flour
Vegetable oil cooking spray

In a small bowl, dissolve yeast in 1/4 cup warm water. In a large bowl, combine milk, melted butter, egg, sugar, salt, pepper, and cheese. Beat until well blended. Stir in yeast mixture. Add flours to milk mixture; beat until smooth. Spray top of dough with cooking spray, cover, and let rise in a warm place (80 to 85 degrees) one hour or until doubled in size.

Stir batter down with a wooden spoon. Spread in a greased 1 1/2-quart round baking dish. Spray top of dough with cooking spray, cover, and let rise 30 minutes or until doubled in size.

Preheat oven to 375 degrees. Bake 25 to 35 minutes or until bread is golden brown and sounds hollow when tapped. Let cool in baking dish 10 minutes. Remove from dish onto a wire rack. Cut into wedges and serve warm.
Yield: 1 loaf bread

BLACK BEAN AND HOMINY SOUP

1 package (16 ounces) chorizo sausage, cooked and drained
2 cans (14 1/2 ounces each) beef broth
2 cans (15 ounces each) black beans, rinsed and drained
1 can (15 1/2 ounces) golden hominy, rinsed and drained
1 can (14 1/2 ounces) Mexican-style stewed tomatoes, undrained
1 cup shredded uncooked potato
1 cup chopped onion
1 can (4 1/2 ounces) chopped green chiles
2 cloves garlic, minced
1 tablespoon chili powder
1 teaspoon ground cumin
1 tablespoon chopped fresh cilantro

In a large Dutch oven over medium-high heat, combine sausage, beef broth, beans, hominy, tomatoes, potato, onion, green chiles, garlic, chili powder, and cumin. Stirring occasionally, bring to a boil. Reduce heat to low; cover and simmer 40 minutes or until onion and potato are tender. Stir in cilantro; serve hot.
Yield: about 10 cups soup

Cheddar Casserole Bread, Black Bean and Hominy Soup

APPLE-CRANBERRY CRUNCH

3 cups cored, unpeeled, and chopped Granny Smith apples
1 can (16 ounces) whole berry cranberry sauce
1/2 cup granulated sugar
1 teaspoon cinnamon
1/4 teaspoon salt
1 cup quick-cooking oats
1/2 cup firmly packed brown sugar
1/3 cup all-purpose flour
1/4 cup chilled butter or margarine
1/2 cup chopped walnuts, toasted

Preheat oven to 350 degrees. In an ungreased 9-inch deep-dish pie plate, combine apples, cranberry sauce, granulated sugar, cinnamon, and salt. In a medium bowl, combine oats, brown sugar, and flour. Using a pastry blender or 2 knives, cut butter into dry ingredients until mixture is crumbly. Stir in walnuts. Sprinkle walnut mixture over apple mixture. Bake 45 to 50 minutes or until golden brown. Serve warm.
Yield: about 8 servings

PUMPKIN PIE CAKE

4 eggs
1 1/2 cups sugar
2 teaspoons ground cinnamon
1 1/2 teaspoons ground nutmeg
1 teaspoon ground ginger
1/4 teaspoon salt
1 can (29 ounces) pumpkin
1 can (12 ounces) evaporated milk
1 package (18 1/4 ounces) yellow cake mix
3/4 cup chilled butter or margarine
1 cup chopped pecans
Whipped cream to garnish

Preheat oven to 350 degrees. In a large bowl, whisk eggs, sugar, cinnamon, nutmeg, ginger, and salt. Stir in pumpkin and evaporated milk. Pour mixture into an ungreased 9 x 13-inch baking pan. Place dry cake mix in a medium bowl. Using a pastry blender or 2 knives, cut butter into cake mix until mixture is crumbly.

Apple-Cranberry Crunch, Pumpkin Pie Cake

Sprinkle cake mixture over pumpkin mixture; sprinkle with pecans. Bake one hour or until top is golden brown and edges start to pull away from sides of pan. Garnish each serving with a dollop of whipped cream. Serve warm.
Yield: about 18 servings

Holiday Candied Corn, Crispy Christmas Trees

Santa's Bundle of Sweets

Everyone will think these unbelievably scrumptious delights came straight from Santa's pack! On these pages, you'll find tempting new confections as well as updated favorites, including chewy molasses cookies and marshmallow sandwich cookies. The Creamy Peanut Butter Fudge is a melt-away marvel not to be missed, and for folks who like their sweets on the crispy side, Holiday Candied Corn and Chocolate Graham Crunch are toothsome tidbits, too. Make plenty of extras and serve these wonderful cookies and candies throughout the Christmas season.

CRISPY CHRISTMAS TREES

1   package (10¹/₂ ounces) miniature marshmallows
¹/₄ cup butter or margarine
12 ounces white candy coating, chopped
¹/₄ teaspoon green liquid food coloring
7   cups crispy rice cereal
    Vegetable oil cooking spray
    White non-pareils to decorate

In a Dutch oven, combine marshmallows and butter. Stirring frequently, cook over low heat until smooth. Add candy coating; stir until smooth. Turn off heat, leaving pan on burner. Tint green. Add cereal; stir until well coated. Spray a 3³/₄ x 4¹/₄-inch tree-shaped plastic mold with cooking spray. Sprinkle non-pareils into mold. Press cereal mixture into mold. Rap mold on a hard surface to release tree. Repeat for remaining trees. Store in a single layer between sheets of waxed paper in an airtight container.

Yield: about 12 trees

HOLIDAY CANDIED CORN

24 cups popped popcorn
1³/₄ cups sugar
1   cup butter or margarine
¹/₂ cup light corn syrup
¹/₂ teaspoon salt
3   cups miniature marshmallows
1   teaspoon almond extract
3   cups green and red fruit-flavored sour candies

Preheat oven to 250 degrees. Place popcorn in a greased large roasting pan. In a heavy large saucepan, combine sugar, butter, corn syrup, and salt over medium heat.

Stirring constantly, bring to a boil. Boil 2 minutes without stirring. Remove from heat. Add marshmallows; stir until melted. Stir in almond extract. Pour marshmallow mixture over popcorn; stir until well coated. Bake one hour; stirring every 15 minutes. Spread on lightly greased aluminum foil to cool. Sprinkle candies over popcorn. Store in an airtight container.

Yield: about 30 cups candied corn

CHRISTMAS ROUNDS

The holly decorations on these cookies are worth the effort; invite a friend to help.

COOKIES

- 6 tablespoons butter or margarine, softened
- 1/2 cup sugar
- 1 egg
- 1/2 teaspoon almond extract
- 1 1/2 cups all-purpose flour
- 1/4 teaspoon baking powder
- 1/4 teaspoon salt

GREEN CANDY

- 2/3 cup sugar
- 1/2 cup water
- 2 tablespoons light corn syrup
- 1/2 teaspoon white vinegar
- 1/8 teaspoon salt
- 1/2 teaspoon almond extract
- 1/8 teaspoon green liquid food coloring

RED CANDY

- 2/3 cup sugar
- 1/2 cup water
- 2 tablespoons light corn syrup
- 1/2 teaspoon white vinegar
- 1/8 teaspoon salt
- 1/2 teaspoon almond extract
- 1/8 teaspoon red liquid food coloring

Christmas Rounds

Preheat oven to 350 degrees. For cookies, line a baking sheet with lightly greased aluminum foil. In a large bowl, cream butter and sugar until fluffy. Add egg and almond extract; beat until smooth. In a small bowl, combine flour, baking powder, and salt. Add dry ingredients to creamed mixture; stir until a soft dough forms. Divide dough in half. On a lightly floured surface, use a floured rolling pin to roll out half of dough to 1/8-inch thickness. Use a 3-inch-diameter scalloped-edge cookie cutter to cut out cookies. Transfer to prepared baking sheet. Use a 1 1/4-inch leaf-shaped cookie cutter to cut 2 leaves in each cookie. Bake 8 to 10 minutes or until bottoms of cookies are lightly browned. Cool cookies on baking sheet 3 minutes; transfer cookies on foil to a wire rack to cool completely.

For green candy, combine sugar, water, corn syrup, vinegar, and salt in a heavy small saucepan. Stirring constantly, cook over medium heat until sugar dissolves. Using a pastry brush dipped in hot water, wash down any sugar crystals on sides of pan. Attach a candy thermometer to pan, making sure thermometer does not touch bottom of pan. Increase heat to medium high and bring to a boil. Cook, without stirring, until mixture reaches 270 degrees. Test about 1/2 teaspoon mixture in ice water. Mixture will form hard threads in ice water but will soften when removed from water. Remove from heat; stir in almond extract and green food coloring (return saucepan to very low heat as necessary to keep candy melted). Spoon about 1/4 teaspoon green candy into each leaf cutout; use a toothpick to pull candy into points of leaves.

For red candy, prepare as for green candy, tinting mixture red. Drop red candy from a toothpick to make 3 "holly berries" on each cookie. Let candy harden; remove cookies from foil. Store in a single layer in an airtight container.

Yield: about 3 dozen cookies

CHOCOLATE GRAHAM CRUNCH

12 chocolate graham crackers
    (2¹/₂ x 4³/₄ inches each)
 2 cups finely chopped peanuts
 1 cup butter
 1 cup firmly packed brown sugar
³/₄ cup semisweet chocolate mini
    chips

Preheat oven to 400 degrees. Arrange graham crackers in a single layer with sides touching in bottom of a greased 10 x 15-inch jellyroll pan. Sprinkle peanuts evenly over crackers. In a heavy small saucepan, combine butter and brown sugar. Stirring constantly, cook over medium heat until sugar dissolves and mixture begins to boil. Continue to boil syrup 3 minutes longer without stirring; pour over crackers. Sprinkle chocolate chips over syrup. Bake 8 to 10 minutes or until top is bubbly. Cool completely in pan. Break into pieces. Store in an airtight container. **Yield:** about 2¹/₄ pounds candy

Christmas Stockings

CHRISTMAS STOCKINGS

COOKIES
 1 cup butter or margarine,
    softened
 1 cup granulated sugar
¹/₂ cup confectioners sugar
 1 egg
 1 teaspoon vanilla extract
2¹/₄ cups all-purpose flour
¹/₄ teaspoon baking powder
¹/₄ teaspoon salt

ICING
 4 cups confectioners sugar
 6 tablespoons water
 3 tablespoons meringue powder
1¹/₂ teaspoons clear vanilla extract
    Green and red paste food
    coloring

Preheat oven to 375 degrees. For cookies, cream butter and sugars in a large bowl until fluffy. Add egg and vanilla; beat until smooth. In a medium bowl, combine flour, baking powder, and salt. Add dry ingredients to creamed mixture; stir until a soft dough forms. On a lightly floured surface, use a floured rolling pin to roll out dough to ¹/₄-inch thickness. Use a 5-inch-high stocking-shaped cookie cutter to cut out cookies. Transfer to a lightly greased baking sheet. Bake 7 to 9 minutes or until edges are lightly browned. Transfer cookies to a wire rack to cool.

For icing, beat confectioners sugar, water, meringue powder, and vanilla in a medium bowl at high speed of an electric mixer 7 to 10 minutes or until stiff. Transfer 1¹/₃ cups icing to a small bowl; tint green. Transfer ¹/₂ cup icing to another small bowl; tint red. Leave remaining icing white. Add additional water to each icing, ¹/₂ teaspoon at a time, until icing flows from a spoon. Spoon each icing into a pastry bag fitted with a small round tip. Outline and fill in cuffs, heels, and toes with white icing. Outline and fill in remainder of cookie with green icing; allow to harden slightly. Pipe white icing decorative lines onto each cookie. Using red icing, pipe name and "stitches" onto each cookie. Let icing harden. Store in an airtight container.
Yield: about 1¹/₂ dozen cookies

Chocolate Graham Crunch

APRICOT-NUT BARS

Dough is tender; using plastic wrap will help shape and move the dough.

DOUGH
- 1/2 cup butter or margarine, softened
- 1/2 cup granulated sugar
- 1/2 cup firmly packed brown sugar
- 1/4 cup honey
- 2 eggs
- 1 teaspoon vanilla extract
- 3 1/4 cups all-purpose flour
- 3/4 teaspoon baking soda
- 1/2 teaspoon salt

FILLING
- 8 ounces finely chopped dried apricots (about 1 1/2 cups)
- 1 1/3 cups water
- 1/2 cup granulated sugar
- 1/2 cup firmly packed brown sugar
- 1/4 cup all-purpose flour
- 2/3 cup finely chopped walnuts
- 3 tablespoons orange juice

For dough, cream butter and sugars in a large bowl until fluffy. Add honey, eggs, and vanilla; beat until smooth. In a medium bowl, combine flour, baking soda, and salt. Add dry ingredients to creamed mixture; stir until a soft dough forms. Divide dough into fourths. Wrap in plastic wrap and chill one hour.

For filling, combine apricots and water in a heavy medium saucepan over medium heat. Stirring occasionally, bring mixture to a boil; boil 5 minutes. In a small bowl, combine sugars and flour; stir into apricot mixture. Reduce heat to medium low. Stirring frequently, cook mixture 10 minutes or until thickened. Remove from heat. Stir in walnuts and orange juice. Transfer to a heatproof container and allow mixture to cool.

Preheat oven to 350 degrees. On a sheet of plastic wrap, use a floured rolling pin to roll out one fourth of

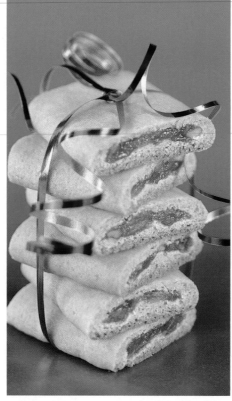

Apricot-Nut Bars

Double Delight Sandwich Cookies

dough into an 8 x 12-inch rectangle. Cut dough crosswise into four 3 x 8-inch pieces. Cut plastic wrap to separate dough pieces. Spread 2 tablespoons apricot mixture down center of each strip of dough. Use plastic wrap to fold long sides of each dough strip over filling, slightly overlapping edges. Using a spatula under plastic wrap to lift dough, place dough strips, seam side down, 2 inches apart on an ungreased baking sheet. Remove plastic wrap. Bake 12 to 14 minutes or until bottoms are lightly browned. Cool cookies on baking sheet 5 minutes; transfer to a wire rack to cool completely.

Transfer cookies to a cutting board; cut into 2-inch-long bars. Repeat with remaining dough. Store in an airtight container.
Yield: about 5 dozen bars

DOUBLE DELIGHT SANDWICH COOKIES

- 1 jar (7 ounces) marshmallow creme
- 1/3 cup smooth peanut butter
- 1 package (12 ounces) round butter-flavored crackers
- 16 ounces chocolate candy coating, chopped
- 1 package (6 ounces) semisweet chocolate chips

In a small bowl, beat marshmallow creme and peanut butter until well blended. Spoon about 1 teaspoon filling onto half of crackers. Place remaining crackers on top of filling; lightly press crackers together. In a heavy medium saucepan, melt candy coating and chocolate chips over low heat. Remove from heat. Place each cracker sandwich on a fork and dip into chocolate, covering completely. Place on waxed paper and allow chocolate to harden. Store in an airtight container in a cool place.
Yield: about 4 dozen sandwich cookies

CREAMY PEANUT BUTTER FUDGE

- 2 cups granulated sugar
- 1 cup firmly packed brown sugar
- 2 cans (5 ounces each) evaporated milk
- 1/2 cup butter or margarine
- 1 1/4 cups smooth peanut butter
- 1 jar (7 ounces) marshmallow creme
- 1 teaspoon vanilla extract

Line a 9-inch square baking pan with aluminum foil, extending foil over 2 sides of pan; grease foil. Butter sides of a very heavy large saucepan. Combine sugars, evaporated milk, and butter in saucepan. Stirring constantly, cook over medium-low heat until sugar dissolves. Using a pastry brush dipped in hot water, wash down any sugar crystals on sides of pan. Attach a candy thermometer to pan, making sure thermometer does not touch bottom of pan. Increase heat to medium and bring to a boil. Cook, stirring occasionally, until mixture reaches soft-ball stage (approximately 234 to 240 degrees). Test about 1/2 teaspoon mixture in ice water. Mixture will easily form a ball in ice water but will flatten when removed from water. Remove from heat and stir in peanut butter, marshmallow creme, and vanilla. Pour into prepared pan. Chill 4 hours or until firm.

Cut into 1-inch squares. Store in an airtight container in a cool place.

Yield: about 6 1/2 dozen pieces fudge

Sweet Molasses Boys

SWEET MOLASSES BOYS

- 1/2 cup butter or margarine, softened
- 1/2 cup firmly packed brown sugar
- 1 egg
- 1/4 cup molasses
- 1/2 teaspoon vanilla extract
- 2 cups all-purpose flour
- 1 teaspoon baking powder
- 1/2 teaspoon ground cinnamon
- 1/8 teaspoon salt
  Raisins, cut in half
  Granulated sugar

In a large bowl, cream butter and brown sugar until fluffy. Add egg, molasses, and vanilla; beat until smooth. In a small bowl, combine flour, baking powder, cinnamon, and salt. Add dry ingredients to creamed mixture; stir until a soft dough forms. Divide dough in half; wrap in plastic wrap. Chill 2 hours or until firm.

Preheat oven to 350 degrees. On a lightly floured surface, use a floured rolling pin to roll out half of dough to 1/4-inch thickness. Use a 4 1/4 x 5 1/4-inch gingerbread boy-shaped cookie cutter to cut out cookies. Transfer to a greased baking sheet. Press raisin halves into cookies for "eyes." Sprinkle cookies with granulated sugar. Bake 8 to 10 minutes or until bottoms are lightly browned. Transfer cookies to a wire rack to cool. Repeat with remaining dough. Store in an airtight container.

Yield: about 10 cookies

Creamy Peanut Butter Fudge

Tasty Muffins, Homemade Sausage

Breakfast
At Your Pace

Awaken your family with the tantalizing aromas of fresh Tasty Muffins and savory Homemade Sausage. Then, for a leisurely holiday breakfast, let them serve themselves Make-Your-Own Omelets, Toasted Granola, and Hot Chocolate Mix. Or pamper your sleepyheads with Corned Beef Hash Casserole or Sweet or Savory Pastries — both melt-in-your-mouth wonders that you can assemble the night before! A perfect side dish for sausage, peppery Baked Tomatoes and Artichokes are surrounded with crispy onions and celery. Sweet and fluffy Frozen Fruit Salads or creamy Breakfast Smoothies are a cool and tangy way to end your relaxed morning.

TASTY MUFFINS

Make the basic muffin recipe or one or more of the variations.

Basic Muffins
1 3/4 cups self-rising flour
3 tablespoons sugar
3/4 cup milk
2 eggs
1/2 cup butter or margarine, melted

Preheat oven to 350 degrees. In a medium bowl, combine flour and sugar. Make a well in center of dry ingredients. In a small bowl, combine milk, eggs, and melted butter; beat until well blended. Add to dry ingredients; stir just until moistened. Spoon 1 tablespoon batter into each greased cup of a miniature muffin pan. Bake 10 to 14 minutes or until a toothpick inserted in center of muffin comes out clean. Cool in pan 5 minutes. Serve warm or cool completely and store in an airtight container.
Yield: about 2 1/2 dozen mini muffins

MUFFIN VARIATIONS:
Mocha-Nut Muffins
Add 1/2 teaspoon vanilla, 1/3 cup mini chocolate chips, melted, and 1 tablespoon instant coffee granules to liquid ingredients. Stir in 3/4 cup mini chocolate chips and 1/2 cup finely chopped toasted pecans.
Yield: about 4 dozen mini muffins

Oatmeal Muffins
Substitute brown sugar for granulated sugar. Substitute 3/4 cup quick-cooking oats for 3/4 cup flour.
Yield: about 3 dozen mini muffins

Cornmeal-Cheese Muffins
Substitute 3/4 cup yellow cornmeal for 3/4 cup flour. Add 1 cup finely shredded sharp Cheddar cheese.
Yield: about 3 dozen mini muffins

Cream Cheese Muffins
1 recipe Basic Muffins
2 packages (3 ounces each) cream cheese, softened
2/3 cup granulated sugar
1/2 teaspoon lemon extract
1/4 teaspoon vanilla extract
1/4 cup firmly packed brown sugar
2 1/2 tablespoons all-purpose flour
3/4 teaspoon ground cinnamon
1 tablespoon butter or margarine, softened

Prepare muffin batter. In a small bowl, beat cream cheese, granulated sugar, and extracts until well blended. In another small bowl, combine brown sugar, flour, and cinnamon; blend in butter until mixture is crumbly. Layer the following into each muffin cup: 1 teaspoon batter, 1 teaspoon cream cheese mixture, 1/2 teaspoon batter, and 1/2 teaspoon brown sugar mixture. Bake following Basic Muffins recipe.
Yield: about 4 dozen mini muffins

HOMEMADE SAUSAGE

1 tablespoon rubbed sage
1 1/2 teaspoons salt
1/2 teaspoon ground black pepper
1/2 teaspoon garlic powder
1/2 teaspoon ground thyme
1/4 to 1/2 teaspoon ground red pepper
1/4 teaspoon ground allspice
2 pounds ground pork OR ground turkey

In a small bowl, combine sage, salt, black pepper, garlic powder, thyme, red pepper, and allspice until blended. Process spice mixture and pork in a large food processor just until blended. Store in an airtight container in refrigerator overnight to let flavors blend.

Shape sausage into an 8 x 10-inch rectangle. Cut into 2-inch squares. Shape each piece of sausage into a 2 1/2-inch-diameter patty. Cook patties in a large skillet over medium heat until thoroughly cooked. Serve warm.
Yield: 20 sausage patties

Preheat oven to 350 degrees. In a large deep skillet, sauté celery and onion in oil over medium heat until tender. Stir in tomatoes, artichoke hearts, sugar, salt, pepper, and croutons. Transfer to a greased 2-quart baking dish. Sprinkle Parmesan cheese over top of casserole. Bake 40 to 45 minutes or until bubbly and lightly browned around the edges. Serve warm.
Yield: 8 to 10 servings

MAKE-YOUR-OWN OMELETS

To save you precious time, let everyone prepare his or her own omelet!

 12 eggs
 3/4 cup water
 3/4 teaspoon salt
 1/4 teaspoon ground black pepper
 10 tablespoons butter, divided

In a medium bowl, beat eggs, water, salt, and pepper until well blended. Cover and store in refrigerator until ready to serve.

For each omelet, melt 1 tablespoon butter in a small skillet over medium heat. Add desired filling ingredients except cheese (see variations below). Sauté until vegetables are tender and meat is heated through; keep warm. Melt 2 teaspoons butter in an 8-inch skillet over medium heat. Add 1/2 cup egg mixture to pan. With spatula, carefully push cooked portion of egg toward center of pan to allow uncooked portion to flow over pan surface, tilting pan as necessary. When egg begins to set in center, fill with desired heated filling and cheese. Using a spatula, fold omelet in half and slide onto plate. Serve warm.
Yield: 6 omelets

Baked Tomatoes and Artichokes, Corned Beef Hash Casserole, Make-Your-Own Omelets

BAKED TOMATOES AND ARTICHOKES

 1 cup chopped celery
 1 cup chopped onion
 1/4 cup olive oil
 2 cans (14 1/2 ounces each) diced tomatoes, undrained
 1 can (14 ounces) artichoke hearts, drained and chopped
 1 tablespoon sugar
 1/2 teaspoon salt
 1/2 teaspoon ground black pepper
 2 1/2 cups seasoned croutons
 2 tablespoons freshly grated Parmesan cheese

VARIATIONS:
 Chopped onion
 Chopped sweet pepper
 Mushroom slices
 Cooked sausage
 Cooked ham
 Cooked bacon
 Shredded cheese

CORNED BEEF HASH CASSEROLE

1/2 cup chopped green pepper
1/2 cup chopped white onion
2 tablespoons butter or margarine
2 cups cubed or finely chopped cooked corned beef
1 package (32 ounces) frozen diced potatoes, thawed
1 can (10 3/4 ounces) cream of celery soup
1 container (8 ounces) sour cream
1/2 cup milk
1/2 teaspoon salt
1/2 teaspoon ground black pepper
2 cups (8 ounces) shredded Cheddar cheese
Green pepper rings to garnish

Preheat oven to 375 degrees. In a medium skillet, sauté 1/2 cup green pepper and onion in butter over medium-high heat until crisp-tender. In a large bowl, combine onion mixture, corned beef, potatoes, soup, sour cream, milk, salt, and black pepper. Spoon into a lightly greased 9 x 13-inch baking dish. Cover and bake 55 to 60 minutes or until bubbly. Uncover and sprinkle cheese around edge of dish. Place green pepper rings in center of casserole. Bake 10 minutes or until cheese melts. Serve warm.
Yield: 10 to 12 servings

BREAKFAST SMOOTHIES

For thicker smoothie, use frozen fruit.

1 cup vanilla or fruit-flavored yogurt
1 cup fruit nectar OR milk
1 cup sliced or chopped fruit, if desired
3 tablespoons flavored syrup, if desired
1 cup ice OR 1/2 cup ice cream

Note: A variety of flavored syrups can be found in gourmet coffee shops. Fruit nectars can be found in cans in the fruit juice section of grocery stores.

Breakfast Smoothies, Toasted Granola

Combine yogurt and fruit nectar or milk in a blender. Add fruit and flavored syrup, if desired. Add ice or ice cream. Cover and blend just until smooth. Serve immediately.
Yield: 2 to 3 cups beverage

GOOD COMBINATIONS:

Strawberry yogurt, strawberry or apple nectar, bananas, strawberries, and vanilla ice cream.

Vanilla yogurt, peach nectar, peaches, amaretto syrup, and ice.

Vanilla yogurt, milk, Irish creme syrup, and coffee ice cream.

Vanilla yogurt, milk, hazelnut syrup, and chocolate ice cream.

TOASTED GRANOLA

4 cups round toasted oat cereal
4 cups graham cereal squares
3 3/4 cups old-fashioned oats
1 cup sunflower kernels
1 cup slivered almonds
3/4 cup firmly packed brown sugar
1/3 cup vegetable oil
6 tablespoons frozen orange juice concentrate, thawed
3 tablespoons honey
Fresh fruit and milk or yogurt to serve

Preheat oven to 300 degrees. In a greased large roasting pan, combine cereals, oats, sunflower kernels, and almonds. In a small bowl, combine brown sugar, oil, orange juice concentrate, and honey; stir until well blended. Pour brown sugar mixture over cereal mixture; stir until well coated. Bake 45 minutes or until golden brown, stirring every 10 minutes. Spread on waxed paper and allow to cool. Store in an airtight container in a cool place. Serve with fresh fruit and milk or yogurt.
Yield: about 14 cups granola

SWEET OR SAVORY PASTRIES

Pastries may be assembled ahead of time and chilled until ready to bake.

HAM AND CHEESE

1 sheet (from a 17.3-ounce package) frozen puff pastry, thawed according to package directions
4 ounces cream cheese, softened
1 egg
1 tablespoon chopped green onion
2 teaspoons prepared mustard
1 cup shredded sharp Cheddar cheese
4 ounces shaved ham

LEMON-ALMOND

1 sheet (from a 17.3-ounce package) frozen puff pastry, thawed according to package directions
1 package (8 ounces) cream cheese, softened
1/3 cup confectioners sugar
1 tablespoon freshly squeezed lemon juice
1 teaspoon grated lemon zest
1 teaspoon almond extract
3/4 cup sliced almonds, toasted

Preheat oven to 375 degrees. For ham and cheese pastry, place pastry sheet between sheets of plastic wrap and roll into a 10 x 15-inch rectangle. Use plastic wrap to transfer dough to a nonstick 14 x 17-inch baking sheet; remove plastic wrap. Beat cream cheese, egg, onion, and mustard in a medium bowl until fluffy. Stir in cheese. Spread cream cheese mixture over pastry to within 3 inches of long edges. Place ham over cheese mixture. Use a knife to make 2-inch-long cuts one inch apart along long edges (**Fig. 1**).
Fig. 1

Sweet or Savory Pastries

Beginning at one short edge and alternating sides, fold pastry strips over filling (**Fig. 2**).
Fig. 2

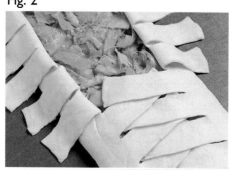

Bake 28 to 30 minutes or until golden brown. Cool in pan 15 minutes. Serve warm or at room temperature.

For lemon-almond pastry, follow ham and cheese instructions to roll out pastry. Beat cream cheese, confectioners sugar, lemon juice, lemon zest, and almond extract in a medium bowl until fluffy. Spread cream cheese mixture over pastry to within 3 inches of long edges. Sprinkle almonds over cream cheese mixture. Continue to follow ham and cheese instructions to fold dough strips and to bake pastry.
Yield: about 10 slices each pastry

HOT CHOCOLATE MIX

Make each cup of hot chocolate to order!

6¼ cups nonfat milk powder
1 jar (16 ounces) non-dairy powdered creamer
1 package (16 ounces) confectioners sugar
1 container (15 ounces) chocolate mix for milk
½ cup cocoa

In a very large bowl, combine all ingredients. Store in an airtight container.

To serve, pour 6 ounces hot water or hot coffee over 2½ heaping tablespoons chocolate mix; stir until well blended. If desired, add one or more of the following variations to each cup of hot chocolate.
Yield: about 14 cups mix

VARIATIONS:

Flavored syrups
Christmas-shaped marshmallows
Ground cinnamon
Flavored coffee creamers

FROZEN FRUIT SALADS

1 jar (6 ounces) maraschino cherries, drained
1 cup sour cream
1 package (3 ounces) cream cheese, softened
1 teaspoon vanilla extract
2 cans (8 ounces each) crushed pineapple, well drained
2 bananas, sliced
½ cup chopped pecans
½ cup whipping cream
½ cup confectioners sugar

Quarter cherries. Drain on a paper towel and pat dry. In a medium bowl, beat sour cream, cream cheese, and vanilla until fluffy. Stir in cherries, pineapple, bananas, and pecans. In a small bowl, beat whipping cream until foamy. Gradually sift confectioners sugar over cream, beating until soft peaks form. Fold into fruit mixture. Spoon into paper-lined muffin cups. Freeze uncovered 1½ hours or until firm. Cover and return to freezer. To serve, let salads thaw at room temperature one hour before serving.
Yield: about 15 servings

Hot Chocolate Mix, Frozen Fruit Salads

Roast Christmas Goose, Wild Rice and Cranberry Dressing, Apricot Chutney

An Elegant Affair

Many of our favorite Yuletide customs are a legacy of the Victorian era. One of these traditions is the Christmas feast with its emphasis on beautiful presentation and a variety of flavors. In honor of the Victorians, we've updated these vintage recipes from the 1860's. Start your dinner with an Appetizer Plate of smoked salmon, cucumber slices, and stuffed celery. Lobster Bisque is a warm and rich delicacy for the first course. For the main course, try a traditional Roast Christmas Goose with the seasonal zest of Wild Rice and Cranberry Dressing. The dessert menu includes Coffee Jelly with whipped cream topping, Toffee Walnuts, and a sumptuous fruitcake. And the frothy Syllabub laced with apple brandy is a rich drink you can serve alone or with other treats either before or after dinner.

WILD RICE AND CRANBERRY DRESSING

- 1/2 cup butter or margarine
- 1 1/2 cups chopped onions
- 3/4 cup thinly sliced celery
- 2 cloves garlic, minced
- 1 package (6 ounces) wild rice
- 1/2 teaspoon dried thyme leaves
- 1/2 teaspoon dried sage leaves
- 1/2 teaspoon salt
- 1/2 teaspoon ground black pepper
- 3 cans (14 1/2 ounces each) chicken broth
- 1 package (16 ounces) brown rice
- 1 package (6 ounces) sweetened dried cranberries
- 1/2 cup chopped fresh parsley
- 1 cup coarsely chopped pecans, toasted

In a heavy Dutch oven, melt butter over medium heat. Sauté onions, celery, and garlic until tender. Stir in wild rice, thyme, sage, salt, and pepper. Add chicken broth; bring to a boil. Reduce heat to low; cover and simmer 30 minutes. Stir in brown rice; cover and continue to simmer 30 minutes. Stir in cranberries and parsley; cover and simmer 20 minutes longer or until broth is absorbed. Stir in pecans. Serve warm.
Yield: about 12 cups dressing

ROAST CHRISTMAS GOOSE

- 1 goose (about 9 1/2 pounds)
- 1 lemon, halved
- Salt
- Ground black pepper
- Pieces of celery and onion

Preheat oven to 400 degrees. Remove giblets and save for another use. Rinse goose and pat dry. Rub outside and inside of goose with lemon. Sprinkle inside and outside of goose with salt and pepper. Place lemon halves, celery, and onion inside goose. Prick the skin all over with a knife. Tie ends of legs to tail with kitchen twine; lift wing tips up and over back so they are tucked under goose. Place goose, breast side up, on a greased rack in a shallow roasting pan. Insert meat thermometer into thickest part of thigh, making sure thermometer does not touch bone. Cook one hour. Turn goose breast side down. Reduce heat to 325 degrees. Continue roasting 1 1/2 to 2 hours or until meat thermometer registers 180 degrees and juices run clear when thickest part of thigh is pierced with a fork. Remove from oven. Transfer goose to a serving platter and let stand 15 minutes before carving. Serve warm.
Yield: 5 to 7 servings

APRICOT CHUTNEY

This is a perfect accompaniment for goose.

- 2 packages (6 ounces each) dried apricots, coarsely chopped
- 1 1/2 cups firmly packed brown sugar
- 1 cup golden raisins
- 1 cup chopped onion
- 1 cup white wine vinegar
- 1 cup apricot nectar
- 1 tablespoon chopped crystallized ginger
- 1 teaspoon salt
- 1/2 teaspoon ground cinnamon
- 1/2 teaspoon mustard seed
- 1/4 teaspoon curry powder

In a heavy large saucepan, combine apricots, brown sugar, raisins, onion, vinegar, apricot nectar, ginger, salt, cinnamon, mustard seed, and curry powder. Stirring frequently, bring mixture to a boil over medium heat. Reduce heat to medium low and simmer uncovered 30 minutes or until fruit is tender and sauce thickens. Remove from heat. Serve warm or at room temperature.
Yield: about 3 1/2 cups chutney

Syllabub, Appetizer Plate

APPETIZER PLATE

SMOKED SALMON

- 1/2 cup sour cream
- 2 tablespoons capers, chopped
- 1 tablespoon chopped fresh dill weed
- 3 ounces smoked salmon, thinly sliced
  Crackers
  Fresh dill weed to garnish

In a small bowl, combine sour cream, capers, and chopped dill weed. Place small pieces of salmon on crackers. Place about 1/2 teaspoon sour cream mixture on each salmon piece. Garnish with dill weed. Serve immediately.

Yield: about 2 dozen appetizers

CUCUMBER SLICES

Topping can be made ahead and chilled.

- 6 hard-cooked eggs, quartered
- 1/4 cup mayonnaise
- 3 tablespoons sour cream
- 2 tablespoons Dijon-style mustard
- 1 tablespoon freshly squeezed lemon juice
- 1/2 cup chopped fresh herbs (we used parsley, tarragon, and thyme)
- 1/2 teaspoon salt
- 1/4 teaspoon ground black pepper
- 2 to 3 cucumbers
  Paprika and fresh parsley to garnish

Process eggs, mayonnaise, sour cream, mustard, and lemon juice in a food processor until smooth. Add herbs, salt, and pepper; process just until blended. Transfer mixture to a pastry bag fitted with a large star tip. Score skins of cucumbers with a fork. Cut into 1/4-inch slices; pat dry. Pipe topping onto each slice. Garnish with paprika and parsley. Chill until ready to serve.

Yield: about 3 1/2 dozen appetizers

STUFFED CELERY

Filling can be made ahead and chilled.

  Celery ribs cut into 3-inch pieces
- 1 package (8 ounces) cream cheese, softened
- 2 tablespoons confectioners sugar
- 1 can (8 ounces) crushed pineapple in juice, finely chopped and drained
- 1/2 cup finely chopped pecans, toasted

Cut off a small amount on bottom of each celery piece so it will sit flat. In a small bowl, beat cream cheese and confectioners sugar until fluffy. Stir in pineapple and pecans. Transfer mixture to a pastry bag fitted with a large round tip. Pipe mixture into center of each celery piece. Chill until ready to serve.

Yield: about 4 dozen appetizers

SYLLABUB

2 cups milk
1 1/2 cups sugar
1/8 teaspoon salt
1 vanilla bean
1 1/4 cups apple cider
3/4 cup apple brandy
2 cups whipping cream, whipped
Freshly grated nutmeg to garnish

In a large saucepan, combine milk, sugar, and salt. Split vanilla bean in half lengthwise. Scrape seeds into milk mixture and add vanilla bean. Stirring frequently, cook over medium heat until sugar dissolves. Remove vanilla bean. Strain mixture through several layers of cheesecloth into a 2-quart container. Stir in apple cider. Chill until ready to serve.

To serve, combine brandy and chilled apple cider mixture in a punch bowl. Fold in whipped cream. Whisk until well blended. Garnish with nutmeg. Serve immediately.
Yield: about 9 cups punch

Lobster Bisque, Fluffy Yeast Rolls

LOBSTER BISQUE

Recipe can be easily doubled.

4 lobster tails
4 cups chicken broth
1 onion, sliced
4 ribs celery with leaves, coarsely chopped
6 black peppercorns
2 whole cloves
1 bay leaf
2/3 cup butter or margarine
2/3 cup all-purpose flour, sifted
3/4 teaspoon salt
4 1/2 cups milk
1 1/2 cups whipping cream
Croutons to garnish

Place lobster tails in a large Dutch oven. Add enough water to cover. Bring to a boil over medium-high heat; cook about 4 minutes or until lobster turns pink. Remove tails and rinse under cold water. Remove lobster meat from shells and cut into small pieces. Cover and chill.

In a large saucepan, combine chicken broth, onion, celery, peppercorns, cloves, and bay leaf.

Bring to a boil over medium-high heat. Reduce heat to medium low; cover and simmer 35 minutes. Strain stock; set aside. Discard vegetables and spices.

Melt butter in a large Dutch oven over medium heat. Whisk in flour and salt. Whisking constantly, gradually add milk; whisk until mixture is smooth. Add chicken stock; bring to a boil. Stir in whipping cream and return to a simmer. Add lobster meat; cover and simmer about 3 minutes or until heated through. Garnish each serving with croutons. Serve warm.
Yield: about 10 cups soup

FLUFFY YEAST ROLLS

2 packages dry yeast
2 cups warm water
4 1/2 to 5 cups all-purpose flour, divided
2 tablespoons sugar
1 teaspoon salt
1/4 cup butter or margarine, melted
Vegetable oil cooking spray

In a small bowl, dissolve yeast in 2 cups warm water. In a large bowl, combine 4 1/2 cups flour, sugar, and salt. Add butter and yeast mixture to dry ingredients; stir until a soft dough forms. Turn onto a lightly floured surface. Knead about 5 minutes or until dough becomes smooth and elastic, using additional flour as necessary. Place in a large bowl sprayed with cooking spray, turning once to coat top of dough. Cover and let rise in a warm place (80 to 85 degrees) one hour or until doubled in size.

Turn dough onto a lightly floured surface and punch down. Separate dough into 24 equal pieces. Shape dough into rolls and place in 2 greased 9-inch square baking pans. Spray tops of dough with cooking spray, cover, and let rise in a warm place 45 minutes or until doubled in size.

Preheat oven to 350 degrees. Bake 18 to 23 minutes or until golden brown. Serve warm.
Yield: 2 dozen rolls

Carrot Ring with Green Peas, Spinach-Stuffed Tomatoes

CARROT RING WITH GREEN PEAS

- 1 pound carrots, peeled, cooked and puréed
- 2 eggs, beaten
- 1/4 cup butter or margarine, melted
- 1 1/2 tablespoons all-purpose flour
- 1 tablespoon sugar
- 2 teaspoons chopped fresh tarragon leaves
- 1 teaspoon salt, divided
- 1 cup half and half
- 2 packages (10 ounces each) frozen small green peas, thawed
- 2 tablespoons butter or margarine
- 2 tablespoons chopped fresh mint leaves

Preheat oven to 350 degrees. In a large bowl, combine carrots, eggs, melted butter, flour, sugar, tarragon, and 1/2 teaspoon salt; stir until well blended. Stir in half and half. Pour mixture into a greased 1-quart ring mold. Place mold in a 9 × 13-inch baking pan; pour hot water into baking pan halfway up sides of mold. Bake 50 to 60 minutes or until mixture is set. Cool in mold 10 minutes. Unmold onto serving plate.

While carrot ring is baking, place peas, butter, remaining 1/2 teaspoon salt, and mint in a microwave-safe bowl. Cover and cook on high power (100%) 10 minutes or until peas are tender, stirring occasionally. Spoon peas into center of warm carrot ring. Serve warm.

Yield: about 8 servings

SPINACH-STUFFED TOMATOES

- 8 firm medium-size tomatoes
- 1/2 cup finely chopped onion
- 2 tablespoons olive oil
- 12 cups chopped fresh ready-to-eat spinach (about two 10-ounce bags)
- 1/4 cup chopped fresh basil leaves
- 3/4 cup purchased plain bread crumbs, divided
- 1/4 cup plus 2 tablespoons freshly grated Parmesan cheese, divided
- 3/4 teaspoon salt
- 1/4 teaspoon ground black pepper

Cut tops from tomatoes. Using a spoon, hollow center of tomatoes removing seeds but leaving pulp around sides of tomato. Invert onto a wire rack to drain.

Preheat oven to 375 degrees. In a large skillet, sauté onion in oil over medium heat until tender. Increase heat to medium high; stir in spinach and basil. Stirring constantly, cook spinach mixture about 2 minutes or until wilted. Stir in 1/2 cup bread crumbs, 1/4 cup cheese, salt, and pepper. Spoon mixture into tomatoes. Place in a greased 9 × 13-inch baking dish. In a small bowl, combine remaining 1/4 cup bread crumbs and 2 tablespoons cheese. Sprinkle about 1 tablespoon mixture on top of each tomato. Bake 20 to 25 minutes or until tomatoes are heated through and topping is lightly browned. Serve warm.

Yield: 8 servings

POTATO CROQUETTES

9 medium red potatoes, peeled and quartered (about 3¹/₂ pounds)
¹/₃ cup butter or margarine, softened
¹/₂ cup finely chopped green onions
3 eggs, beaten
1 teaspoon salt
¹/₄ teaspoon ground white pepper
1 cup purchased seasoned bread crumbs
Vegetable oil

In a Dutch oven, cover potatoes with salted water. Bring water to a boil; reduce heat, cover, and cook until potatoes are tender. Drain potatoes. Add butter; beat or mash until potatoes are smooth. Let potatoes cool 20 minutes or until cool enough to shape into patties.

Stir in onions, eggs, salt, and white pepper. Place bread crumbs on a plate. Spoon ¹/₃ cup potato mixture at a time onto bread crumbs and shape into a 3-inch-diameter patty, covering with crumbs. In a large skillet, heat a thin layer of oil. Fry patties in oil until golden brown on both sides, adding oil as needed. Serve warm.
Yield: about 18 potato patties

RED AND GREEN CABBAGE MEDLEY

RED CABBAGE
2 tablespoons butter or margarine
¹/₄ cup firmly packed brown sugar
2 tablespoons cider vinegar
1 teaspoon salt
¹/₂ teaspoon ground black pepper
12 cups red cabbage, shredded (about a 2-pound cabbage)
2 Granny Smith apples, peeled, cored, and thinly sliced
¹/₃ cup finely chopped onion

GREEN CABBAGE
5 slices bacon, thinly sliced crosswise
1 teaspoon caraway seed
¹/₂ teaspoon salt
¹/₄ teaspoon ground black pepper
1 bay leaf

Red and Green Cabbage Medley, Potato Croquettes

14 cups green cabbage, shredded (about a 2-pound cabbage)
¹/₃ cup finely chopped onion
1 green pepper, cut into 2-inch slivers
¹/₄ cup chicken broth

For red cabbage, melt butter in a large deep skillet over medium-high heat. Stir in brown sugar, vinegar, salt, and pepper. Add cabbage, apples, and onion; stir until well blended. Cover and cook 5 minutes or until cabbage is tender; stirring occasionally.

For green cabbage, cook bacon in a large deep skillet over medium-high heat until crisp. Remove bacon, reserving drippings in skillet. Drain bacon, crumble, and set aside. To drippings, stir in caraway seed, salt, black pepper, and bay leaf. Add cabbage, onion, and green pepper; stir until well blended. Add chicken broth. Cover and cook 5 minutes or until cabbage is tender, stirring occasionally. Remove bay leaf. Stir in bacon. Spoon red and green cabbage into a large bowl. Serve warm.
Yield: 12 to 15 servings each cabbage

TOFFEE WALNUTS

1 pound walnut halves (about
    4½ cups)
1 cup butter
1 cup sugar
⅓ cup water
1 tablespoon light corn syrup
¼ teaspoon salt
1 teaspoon vanilla extract
    Salt

Preheat oven to 350 degrees. Bake walnuts on a baking sheet about 8 minutes or until lightly toasted, stirring after 4 minutes. Turn off oven. Cover toasted walnuts with aluminum foil on baking sheet. Return to oven to stay warm.

Line another baking sheet with aluminum foil; grease foil. Butter sides of a very heavy large saucepan. Combine butter, sugar, water, corn syrup, and salt in saucepan. Stirring constantly, cook over medium-low heat until sugar dissolves. Using a pastry brush dipped in hot water, wash down any sugar crystals on sides of pan. Attach a candy thermometer to pan, making sure thermometer does not touch bottom of pan. Increase heat to medium and bring to a boil. Cook, without stirring, until mixture reaches hard-crack stage (approximately 300 to 310 degrees). Test about ½ teaspoon mixture in ice water. Mixture will form brittle threads in ice water and will remain brittle when removed from water. Remove from heat and stir in warm walnuts and vanilla. Spread mixture onto prepared baking sheet; sprinkle with salt. Using 2 forks, pull walnuts apart on baking sheet. Let walnuts cool. Store in an airtight container.
Yield: about 7½ cups walnuts

Coffee Jelly, Toffee Walnuts

COFFEE JELLY

¾ cup granulated sugar
¾ cup coffee-flavored liqueur
¼ cup cold water
2 envelopes unflavored gelatin
4 cups very strong hot coffee
½ cup whipping cream
1 tablespoon confectioners sugar

In a heatproof medium bowl, combine granulated sugar, liqueur, and water. Sprinkle gelatin over top of mixture; let stand 5 minutes. Add hot coffee; stir until granulated sugar and gelatin dissolve. Cool 15 minutes.

Pour mixture into individual serving dishes. Cover and chill about 2 hours or until firm.

To serve, beat whipping cream and confectioners sugar in a medium bowl until stiff peaks form. Place a dollop of whipped cream on each serving.
Yield: about 10 servings

Homer's Award-Winning Fruitcake

HOMER'S AWARD-WINNING FRUITCAKE

- 1 container (8 ounces) red candied cherries, divided
- 1 container (8 ounces) green candied cherries, divided
- 2½ cups pecan halves, divided
- 1 container (16 ounces) diced mixed candied fruit
- 1 container (16 ounces) glazed pineapple
- 1 package (8 ounces) chopped dates
- 1 container (4 ounces) diced candied orange peel
- 1 container (4 ounces) diced lemon peel
- 1½ cups chopped walnuts
- 1 cup water
- 3½ cups all-purpose flour, divided
- 2 cups butter or margarine, softened
- 1½ cups sugar
- 1½ cups light corn syrup, divided
- 6 eggs
- 1 teaspoon salt

Grease a 10-inch tube pan with a removable bottom; set aside. Preheat oven to 300 degrees. Reserve 10 each of red and green cherries and ½ cup pecans to decorate cake. Slice reserved cherries in half; set aside.

In a large bowl, combine remaining cherries, remaining 2 cups pecans, mixed fruit, pineapple, dates, orange peel, lemon peel, walnuts, and water; stir until well mixed. Stirring frequently, let stand 10 minutes or until water is absorbed. Stir in 2 cups flour. Mix until all of fruit and nuts are evenly coated. In another large bowl, beat butter, sugar, and ½ cup corn syrup until fluffy. Add eggs, salt, and remaining 1½ cups flour; beat until well combined. Combine fruit mixture with batter, stirring until well combined. Spoon batter into pan, packing down to avoid air pockets. Bake about 2¾ hours or until a wooden skewer inserted in center of cake comes out clean. (Cover cake with foil if it begins to brown too quickly.) Cool completely in pan on a wire rack (about 4 hours). Remove cake from pan and place on a serving plate.

In a small saucepan, bring remaining 1 cup corn syrup to a boil over medium heat; cook one minute. Brush hot syrup over top of cake. Decorate with reserved cherries and pecans. Brush top and sides of cake, including fruit and pecans, with remaining syrup. Store in an airtight container.

Yield: about 30 servings

Double Chocolate Christmas Cake

STAR OF WONDER

To match all the grandeur of the season, serve these heavenly confections! Beneath the rich frostings of the Double Chocolate Christmas Cake are layers of tempting white and dark chocolate cake. The Golden Lemon Stars are celestial sweets adorned with golden trims and lacy swirls of icing. Layered Apricot Delight will dazzle taste buds to tangy perfection, while Chocolate Petite Cheesecakes with cherry topping will make a stellar ending to your holiday celebrations.

DOUBLE CHOCOLATE CHRISTMAS CAKE

CAKE
- 1 1/2 cups butter or margarine, softened
- 2 1/4 cups sugar
- 4 eggs, separated
- 1 tablespoon vanilla extract
- 3 1/2 cups all-purpose flour
- 1 1/2 teaspoons baking powder
- 1 teaspoon baking soda
- 1/2 teaspoon salt
- 2 cups buttermilk
- 1 cup chopped pecans, toasted
- 3 ounces white baking chocolate, melted
- 6 ounces semisweet baking chocolate, melted

FROSTING
- 1/2 cup butter or margarine, softened
- 11 ounces cream cheese, softened
- 4 ounces white baking chocolate, melted and cooled
- 5 1/2 cups confectioners sugar

GLAZE
- 3 tablespoons whipping cream
- 3 ounces semisweet baking chocolate, finely chopped
- 2 tablespoons butter or margarine

Preheat oven to 350 degrees. For cake, grease three 9-inch round cake pans. Line bottom of pans with waxed paper; grease waxed paper. Lightly flour pans. In a large bowl, cream butter and sugar until fluffy. Add egg yolks and vanilla; beat until smooth. In a medium bowl, combine flour, baking powder, baking soda, and salt. Alternately beat dry ingredients and buttermilk into creamed mixture, beating until well blended. Stir in pecans. In a medium bowl, beat egg whites until stiff peaks form; fold into batter. Transfer 3 cups batter to a medium bowl; stir in melted white chocolate. Stir melted semisweet chocolate into remaining batter. Spread semisweet batter into 2 prepared pans. Spread white chocolate batter into remaining prepared pan. Bake 30 to 35 minutes or until a toothpick inserted in center of cake comes out clean. Cool in pans 10 minutes. Remove from pans and cool completely on a wire rack. Carefully remove waxed paper.

For frosting, cream butter and cream cheese in a large bowl until fluffy. Add melted white chocolate and beat until well blended. Gradually add confectioners sugar, beating until smooth. Place one dark cake layer on a serving plate; spread top of layer with about 1/2 cup frosting. Repeat with light cake layer. Top with remaining dark cake layer. Spread remaining frosting over top and sides of cake.

For glaze, place whipping cream in a small microwave-safe bowl. Microwave on high power (100%) just until it begins to boil. Add chocolate and butter; stir until glaze is smooth, thick, and glossy. Pour glaze in center of cake, spreading until glaze runs down sides of cake. Let glaze harden. Store in an airtight container in refrigerator.

Yield: about 16 servings

Golden Lemon Stars

BELLINI

- 1 can (12½ ounces) peach nectar
- 3 tablespoons freshly squeezed lemon juice
- 1 to 2 tablespoons grenadine syrup
- 1 bottle (750 ml) champagne, chilled
  Fresh or frozen whole strawberries, red raspberries, and peach wedges

Pour peach nectar, lemon juice, and grenadine into a 1½-quart pitcher. Stir in champagne. Place fruit in serving glasses and add champagne mixture. Serve immediately.
Yield: about 5 cups bellini

CHOCOLATE PETITE CHEESECAKES

CRUST
- 1¾ cups chocolate graham cracker crumbs (about twelve 2½ x 5-inch crackers)
- ¼ cup butter or margarine, softened
- 2 tablespoons sugar

FILLING
- 2 packages (8 ounces each) cream cheese, softened
- ¾ cup sugar
- 4 eggs
- 1 package (12 ounces) semisweet chocolate chips, melted
- 1 cup whipping cream
- 1 teaspoon vanilla extract
- 1 can (21 ounces) cherry pie filling

Line a muffin pan with aluminum foil muffin cups. For crust, combine graham cracker crumbs, butter, and sugar in a medium bowl. Press a tablespoonful of mixture into bottom of each muffin cup.

Preheat oven to 350 degrees. For filling, beat cream cheese in a large bowl until fluffy. Gradually beat in sugar. Add eggs, one at a time, beating well after each addition. Beat in melted chocolate chips. Add whipping cream and vanilla; beat until smooth. Spoon about ¼ cup filling over crust in each muffin cup. Bake

GOLDEN LEMON STARS

COOKIES
- ½ cup butter or margarine, softened
- ½ cup granulated sugar
- ½ cup confectioners sugar
- 1 egg
- 1 teaspoon lemon extract
- 1 teaspoon vanilla extract
- ½ teaspoon yellow food coloring
- 1¾ cups all-purpose flour
- ½ teaspoon baking powder
- ¼ teaspoon ground cardamom
- ¼ teaspoon salt

ICING
- 2 tablespoons vegetable shortening
- 2 tablespoons butter or margarine, softened
- 1 teaspoon lemon extract
- 1 cup confectioners sugar
- 1 teaspoon water
  Gold dragées for decoration only

For cookies, cream butter and sugars in a large bowl until fluffy. Add egg, extracts, and food coloring; beat until smooth. In a medium bowl, combine flour, baking powder, cardamom, and salt. Add dry ingredients to creamed mixture; stir until a soft dough forms. Divide dough in half. Wrap dough in plastic wrap and chill 2 hours or until dough is firm.

Preheat oven to 350 degrees. On a lightly floured surface, use a floured rolling pin to roll out half of dough to slightly less than ⅛-inch thickness. Use a 3½-inch star-shaped cookie cutter to cut out cookies. Transfer to a greased baking sheet. Use a 1¾-inch star-shaped cookie cutter to cut out centers of cookies. Remove centers from cookies. Bake 6 to 8 minutes or until lightly browned on bottom. Cool cookies on baking sheet 2 minutes; transfer to a wire rack to cool. Repeat with remaining dough.

For icing, beat shortening, butter, and lemon extract in a small bowl until fluffy. Add confectioners sugar and water; beat until smooth. Spoon icing into a pastry bag fitted with a small round tip. Pipe outline and decorative pattern onto cookies. Use dots of icing to attach dragées to star points. Allow icing to harden. Store in an airtight container. Remove dragées before eating.
Yield: about 3 dozen cookies

130

Bellini, Chocolate Petite Cheesecakes

18 to 22 minutes or until centers are set. Cool in muffin pan. Remove cheesecakes from pan; chill overnight.

To serve, spoon 1 tablespoon pie filling in center of each cheesecake.

Yield: about 2 dozen cheesecakes

LAYERED APRICOT DELIGHT

1 cup all-purpose flour
1/2 cup butter or margarine, softened
1/2 cup chopped walnuts
3/4 cup granulated sugar
2 tablespoons cornstarch
1 package (3 ounces) apricot gelatin
2 cans (15 1/4 ounces each) apricot halves in heavy syrup
1 package (8 ounces) cream cheese, softened
1 cup confectioners sugar
1 teaspoon vanilla extract
1 cup whipping cream, whipped

Preheat oven to 350 degrees. In a medium bowl beat flour and butter until blended. Stir in walnuts. Spread mixture into bottom of a greased 9 x 13-inch baking dish. Bake 25 minutes or until golden brown. Cool in dish on a wire rack.

In a medium saucepan, combine granulated sugar, cornstarch, and gelatin. Reserving juice, drain and slice apricots. Add enough water to reserved apricot juice to make 1 3/4 cups. Stir juice mixture into sugar mixture. Stirring constantly, cook over medium heat until mixture thickens and becomes clear (about 15 minutes). Cool to room temperature.

Stir apricots into gelatin mixture. In a medium bowl, beat cream cheese, confectioners sugar, and vanilla until fluffy. Fold in whipped cream. Spread cream cheese mixture over cooled crust. Spoon apricot mixture over cream cheese layer. Cover and chill 4 hours or until set.

To serve, cut into 3-inch squares. Store in an airtight container in refrigerator.

Yield: about 12 servings

Layered Apricot Delight

Almond Surprises in Small Shaker Boxes, Marinated Winter Fruit in Fruit Basket

GIFTS
from the Kitchen

This Christmas, let them eat cheesecake! Here's a bounty of fabulous foods, all beautifully presented in cheery baskets, bags, or boxes for holiday gift-giving. With the cooling zing of mint, delicate Peppermint Shortbread is cleverly wrapped to resemble a candy treat. The festive Fruit Basket holds an assortment of cheese and crackers — the perfect companions for a jar of Marinated Winter Fruit. And for the sweetest on your list, Candy Bar Cheesecake is a chocolate lover's dream.

MARINATED WINTER FRUIT

- 3 cups water
- 2 cups dry red wine
- 1/2 cup sugar
- 1/4 cup freshly squeezed lemon juice
- 1 teaspoon grated lemon zest
- 2 cinnamon sticks
- 2 cardamom pods, crushed
- 1 package (12 ounces) lemon-flavored prunes
- 1 package (6 ounces) dried apricots
- 1 package (6 ounces) sweetened dried cranberries
- Cheese and crackers or cookies to serve

In a large saucepan, combine water, wine, sugar, lemon juice, lemon zest, cinnamon sticks, and cardamom. Stirring constantly, bring to a boil over medium-high heat. Reduce heat; simmer 15 minutes, stirring occasionally. In a 1-gallon heatproof container, combine prunes, apricots, and cranberries. Pour hot syrup through a strainer over fruit mixture. Cool to room temperature. Cover and chill overnight to let flavors blend.

Serve at room temperature with cheese and crackers or cookies. Store in an airtight container in refrigerator.
Yield: about 7 cups fruit

Fruit Basket

You will need a hot glue gun, artificial greenery (we used pine stems, holly leaves with berries, and rose leaves), basket with handle (we used a 12" x 15" oval basket), 1 1/3 yds. of 3"w wired ribbon, wood-tone spray, assorted miniature artificial fruits, and tissue paper.

1. Arrange and glue greenery along handle of basket.
2. Lightly apply wood-tone spray to fruits; allow to dry. Leaving space at top of handle for bow, arrange and glue fruits along handle.
3. Refer to *Making a Bow*, page 157, to make a bow with two 6" loops, two 7" loops, a center loop, and two 10" streamers. Arrange and glue bow and streamers along handle of basket.
4. Line basket with tissue paper. Place gift in basket.

ALMOND SURPRISES

- 1 package (14 ounces) flaked coconut
- 1 can (14 ounces) sweetened condensed milk
- 1/2 cup whole almonds, toasted
- 1 package (12 ounces) semisweet chocolate chips
- 8 ounces chocolate candy coating, chopped

In a medium bowl, combine coconut and sweetened condensed milk. With greased hands, shape 1 tablespoon mixture into a ball around each almond. Place on a waxed paper-covered baking sheet and freeze one hour or until firm.

In a medium saucepan, melt chocolate chips and candy coating over low heat. Working with 12 frozen candies at a time, dip into chocolate. Transfer back to baking sheet; chill 15 minutes or until chocolate hardens. Store in single layers between sheets of waxed paper in refrigerator.
Yield: about 4 dozen candies

Small Shaker Boxes

For each box, you will need a small papier-mâché box with tin lid; red, green, and tan acrylic paint; compressed craft sponges; hot glue gun; artificial evergreen sprig with pinecones; artificial red berry sprig; and a small artificial poinsettia.

Refer to Painting Techniques, page 157, before beginning project. Allow paint to dry after each application.

1. Remove lid from box; set aside. Paint bottom and sides of box tan. Lightly sponge paint sides of box red, then green.
2. Glue evergreen sprig, berry sprig, and poinsettia to lid.
3. Place gift in box; replace lid on box.

Apricot-Pineapple Galettes in Tissue-Covered Box

APRICOT-PINEAPPLE GALETTES

It is best to give these cookies the day they are made.

  1 cup butter or margarine,
       softened
  1 cup sugar
  1 egg
  2 teaspoons vanilla extract
2¼ cups all-purpose flour
  1 teaspoon baking powder
 ¼ teaspoon salt
      Sugar
 ⅔ cup apricot preserves
 ⅔ cup pineapple preserves

Preheat oven to 375 degrees. In a large bowl, cream butter and 1 cup sugar until fluffy. Add egg and vanilla; beat until smooth. In a medium bowl, combine flour, baking powder, and salt. Add dry ingredients to creamed mixture; stir until a soft dough forms.

Shape teaspoonfuls of dough into balls and place 2 inches apart on an ungreased baking sheet. Flatten balls into 2-inch-diameter cookies with bottom of a glass dipped in sugar. Bake 5 to 7 minutes or until edges are lightly browned. Transfer cookies to a wire rack to cool.

In a small bowl, combine preserves. Spread about 1 teaspoon preserves on flat side of half the cookies. Press remaining cookies on top of preserves and press lightly to form sandwiches. Store in an airtight container.

Yield: about 3½ dozen galettes

Tissue-Covered Box

You will need an 11" dia. papier-mâché box with lid, red acrylic paint, paintbrush, spray adhesive, Christmas-motif tissue paper, tacky glue, 2⅓ yds. of ⅝"w grosgrain ribbon, craft wire, and an artificial greenery pick.

Allow glue to dry after each application.

1. Remove lid from box. Paint bottom of box red; allow to dry.
2. Lightly draw around lid on wrong side of tissue paper; cut out circle 3" outside drawn line. Lightly crumple tissue paper; smooth out. Apply spray adhesive to top and sides of lid. Gluing excess to inside, smooth tissue paper onto lid.
3. Cut two 14" lengths of ribbon. Crossing ribbons at center, glue ribbons to lid; glue ends to inside of lid.
4. Use remaining ribbon and follow *Making a Bow*, page 157, to make a bow with ten 4" loops and two 4" streamers. Glue bow to center of ribbons on box. Glue greenery to center of bow.

Noel Cakes

PINEAPPLE POUND CAKES

CAKE
- 1 cup butter or margarine, softened
- 1 1/2 cups sugar
- 4 eggs
- 2 cups all-purpose flour
- 1 teaspoon baking powder
- 1/2 teaspoon salt
- 1/2 cup milk
- 2 teaspoons pineapple extract

GLAZE
- 1 can (8 1/4 ounces) crushed pineapple in heavy syrup, drained
- 1 cup sugar
- 1/4 cup butter or margarine
- 1 teaspoon pineapple extract

Preheat oven to 350 degrees. For cake, cream butter and sugar in a large bowl until fluffy. Add eggs, one at a time, beating well after each addition. In a medium bowl, combine flour, baking powder, and salt. Alternately beat dry ingredients and milk into creamed mixture, beating until well blended. Stir in pineapple extract. Spoon batter into 2 greased and floured 4 1/2 x 8 1/2-inch loaf pans. Bake 40 to 50 minutes or until a toothpick inserted in center of cake comes out clean. Cool in pans 5 minutes. Remove from pans and cool completely on a wire rack.

For glaze, combine pineapple, sugar, and butter in a small saucepan. Stirring constantly, cook over medium heat until mixture boils. Stirring frequently, continue to cook about 7 minutes or until mixture begins to thicken. Remove from heat and stir in pineapple extract. Cool 5 minutes or until glaze thickens. Spoon over tops of cakes and cool. Store in an airtight container.
Yield: 2 cakes

Noel Bag
You will need a 10" x 32" piece of red polar fleece, paper-backed fusible web, assorted fabrics, white felt, red embroidery floss, colored

Pineapple Pound Cake in Noel Bag

cellophane, clear tape, and 40" of 3/8" dia. white cotton cord.

1. For bag, match short edges and fold fleece in half. Use a 1/4" seam allowance to stitch long edges of bag together. Turn bag right side out.
2. Use patterns, page 155, and follow *Making Appliqués*, page 156, to make one of each letter appliqué from fabrics. Make one 6 1/4" x 7 1/2" background appliqué with wavy edges from white felt (do not remove paper backing).
3. Arrange and fuse letters to background. Remove paper backing from background; fuse to bag.
4. Stitching through background and front of bag only, use six strands of floss to work *Running Stitch*, page 158, along edges of background.
5. Wrap gift in cellophane and tape to secure. Place gift in bag. Knot ends of cord; tie cord around top of bag.

PEPPERMINT SHORTBREAD

1 cup butter, softened
1/4 cup granulated sugar
1/4 cup finely ground peppermint candies
2 cups all-purpose flour
1/2 cup plus 2 tablespoons confectioners sugar
1 tablespoon half and half
Red paste food coloring

Preheat oven to 325 degrees. In a large bowl, cream butter, granulated sugar, and candies until fluffy. Gradually add flour and stir just until blended (do not overmix). Divide dough into thirds. Pat each third of dough into a 6-inch-diameter circle on a baking sheet lined with parchment paper. Score each round into 8 wedges. Using a fork, prick tops of dough several times. Bake 18 to 23 minutes or until edges are lightly browned. Transfer baking sheets to wire racks; cool 10 minutes. Transfer each piece of parchment paper with shortbread onto a hard cutting surface. Cut each round as scored; cool completely.

In a small bowl, combine confectioners sugar and half and half; stir until smooth. Tint red. Spoon icing into a pastry bag fitted with a small round tip. Pipe icing onto every other shortbread wedge to resemble a peppermint candy. Allow icing to harden. Store in an airtight container.
Yield: 3 shortbread rounds, 8 servings each

Peppermint Packaging
For each package, you will need a 6" dia. cardboard cake circle, clear plastic wrap, clear tape, clear cellophane, and red and green curling ribbons.

1. Tightly cover cardboard circle with plastic wrap; tape at back of circle to secure.
2. Cut a 16" square from cellophane.
3. Place shortbread on plastic-covered cardboard. Overlapping edges at back of cardboard as necessary, wrap cellophane around cardboard to form a tube; use tape to secure.
4. Knot several strands of ribbon together around each end; curl ribbon ends.

Peppermint Shortbread in Peppermint Packaging

Fantastic Fudge

Vanilla-Nut Fudge in White Bags with Bells

VANILLA-NUT FUDGE

2 cups sugar
1 cup evaporated milk
2 tablespoons light corn syrup
1/8 teaspoon salt
1/4 cup butter or margarine
2 teaspoons vanilla extract
3/4 cup chopped walnuts, toasted

Line an 8-inch square baking pan with aluminum foil, extending foil over 2 sides of pan; grease foil. Butter sides of a very heavy large saucepan. Combine sugar, evaporated milk, corn syrup, and salt in saucepan. Stirring constantly, cook over medium-low heat until sugar dissolves. Using a pastry brush dipped in hot water, wash down any sugar crystals on sides of pan. Attach a candy thermometer to pan, making sure thermometer does not touch bottom of pan. Increase heat to medium and bring to a boil. Cook, without stirring, until mixture reaches soft-ball stage (approximately 234 to 240 degrees). Test about 1/2 teaspoon mixture in ice water. Mixture will easily form a ball in ice water but will flatten when removed from water. Place pan in 2 inches of cold water in sink. Add butter and vanilla; do not stir. Cool to approximately 110 degrees. Remove from sink. Using medium speed of an electric mixer, beat about 5 minutes or until fudge thickens. Stir in walnuts. Pour into prepared pan. Cool completely.

Use ends of foil to lift fudge from pan. Cut into 1-inch squares. Store in an airtight container in refrigerator.
Yield: about 4 dozen pieces fudge

White Bags with Bells

For each bag, you will need 12" of 1/16" dia. green wired cord, 1"h bell, artificial greenery stem, white gift bag (we used a 5" x 7" bag made from handmade paper), hot glue gun, and a 15" length of 1 1/2"w wired ribbon.

1. Use cord to attach bell to greenery stem about 1" from end. Glue stem to top front of bag; curl cord ends.
2. Tie ribbon into a bow; notch ends. Glue knot of bow to bag above bell, covering stem.

Lemon Sensation

ZIPPY LEMON SAUCE

3/4 cup sugar
2 tablespoons cornstarch
1/4 teaspoon salt
1 1/2 cups water
2 egg yolks, beaten
1/4 cup butter or margarine, cut into pieces
1/3 cup freshly squeezed lemon juice
1 teaspoon grated lemon zest
Cake or fruit to serve

In top of a double boiler, combine sugar, cornstarch, and salt. Add water; whisk until well blended. Place top of double boiler directly on burner over medium heat. Whisking constantly, bring mixture to a boil; cook 2 minutes or until thickened. Place mixture over bottom of double boiler containing simmering water. Whisking constantly, add a small amount of hot mixture to egg yolks; whisk egg mixture back into hot mixture. Continue to whisk and cook mixture 2 minutes longer. Remove from heat; whisk in butter until melted. Whisk in lemon juice and lemon zest. Serve sauce warm over cake or fruit. Store in an airtight container in refrigerator.
Yield: about 2 cups sauce

Decorative Basket

You will need floral wire; wire cutters; hot glue gun; artificial miniature ivy pick, small lemons, red berry sprig with leaves, and a small evergreen branch; basket with handle (we used a 6 1/2" x 14" basket); 30" length of 1 1/2"w wired ribbon; and a fabric piece to fit in basket.

1. Use wire and hot glue to secure ivy, lemons, and berry sprig on evergreen branch. Arrange branch on handle of basket; use lengths of wire to secure branch in place. Tie ribbon into a bow around branch and handle.
2. For basket liner, fringe edges of fabric 3/4". Place liner, then gift in basket.

Zippy Lemon Sauce in Decorative Basket

Cheesecake Supreme

Candy Bar Cheesecake on Painted Tin Plate

CANDY BAR CHEESECAKE

CRUST
- 1½ cups chocolate graham cracker crumbs
- 6 tablespoons butter, melted
- 2 tablespoons sugar

FILLING
- 4 packages (8 ounces each) cream cheese, softened
- 1 cup firmly packed brown sugar
- 3 eggs
- 1 teaspoon vanilla extract
- 2 chocolate-covered caramel, peanut, and nougat candy bars (2.07 ounces each), chopped
- 2 tablespoons caramel ice-cream topping

Preheat oven to 350 degrees. Wrap aluminum foil under and around outside of a 9-inch springform pan. For crust, combine cracker crumbs, melted butter, and sugar in a medium bowl; stir until well blended. Press into bottom and halfway up sides of prepared pan. Bake 5 minutes; cool completely.

Preheat oven to 350 degrees. For filling, beat cream cheese in a large bowl until fluffy. Gradually beat in brown sugar. Add eggs, one a time, beating well after each addition. Stir in vanilla. Pour batter over crust. Bake one hour or until filling is set. Sprinkle with chopped candy bars. Bake 7 minutes or until candy softens. Cool on a wire rack. Remove sides of pan. Drizzle with caramel topping. Store in an airtight container in refrigerator. **Yield:** 10 to 12 servings

Painted Tin Plate

You will need grey spray primer, 12" dia. tin plate with 2"w rim, masking tape, stencil to fit on rim of plate, palette knife, textured snow medium, brown and metallic bronze acrylic paint, paintbrushes, natural sponge, and clear matte water-based polyurethane satin varnish.

Allow primer, artificial snow, paint, and varnish to dry after each application. Hand wash only and use a soft cloth to dry.

1. Apply primer to plate.
2. Tape stencil to rim of plate. Use palette knife to apply a ¹/₁₆" thick even layer of snow over stencil. Carefully remove stencil; repeat for remaining stenciled areas.
3. Paint plate brown. Referring to *Painting Techniques*, page 157, sponge paint plate bronze. Apply two to three coats of varnish to plate.

3. Use utility knife to cut a piece of floral foam to fit in bottom of flowerpot; glue to secure.

4. Apply primer to star. Paint star yellow. Use utility scissors to cut desired length from dowel. Lightly apply wood-tone spray to star and dowel. Glue end of dowel to back of star. Glue opposite end of dowel in floral foam to secure.

5. Tie 1¹/₂"w ribbon length into a bow around dowel. Fill top of flowerpot with excelsior.

NAPKIN AND NAPKIN RING SET

(Shown on page 73)

For each set, you will need a 16" square of fabric for napkin, 8" of medium-gauge craft wire, and a garland with removable beads.

1. For napkin, fringe edges of fabric square ¹/₂".

2. For napkin ring, remove beads from garland. Thread beads onto center of wire length to within ¹/₂" of each end of wire. Twist ends of wire together to secure and fold to one side.

3. Fold napkin as desired. Place napkin in ring.

PATCHWORK TABLE RUNNER

(Shown on page 73)

For a 16" x 41" table runner, you will need thirty 2" x 22" strips of assorted print fabrics, 18" x 43" piece each of batting and fabric for backing, large darning needle, and embroidery floss.

For all sewing, place right sides together and use a ¹/₄" seam allowance unless otherwise indicated. Press seam allowances to one side.

1. Matching long edges, sew ten fabric strips together to make strip set. Make three strip sets. Cut across strip sets at 2" intervals to make 27 strip units. Alternating order, sew strip units

together to make table runner top.

2. Place backing wrong side up on a flat surface. Place batting, then table runner top, right side up on backing. Baste layers together.

3. To tie table runner, thread darning needle with six strands of floss. Beginning at center of table runner and working toward outside edges, and spacing ties evenly, make a small stitch through all layers at each tie location. Tie floss in a square knot close to fabric; trim ends to 1" from knot.

4. For binding, cut a 2¹/₂" x 3¹/₂ yard print fabric strip, piecing as necessary. Matching wrong sides and raw edges, press strip in half lengthwise. Press one end of binding diagonally (Fig. 1).

Fig. 1

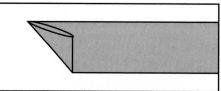

5. Beginning with pressed end several inches from one corner, lay binding around table runner to make sure that seams in binding will not end up at a corner. Adjust placement if necessary. Matching raw edges of binding to raw edges of table runner, pin binding to right side of table runner along one edge.

6. When you reach the first corner, mark ¹/₄" from corner of table runner top (Fig. 2).

Fig. 2

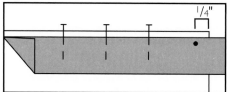

7. Sew binding to table runner top, backstitching at beginning of stitching and when you reach the mark (Fig. 3). Lift needle out of fabric and clip thread.

Fig. 3

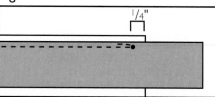

8. Fold binding as shown in Figs. 4 and 5 and pin binding to adjacent side, matching raw edges. When you reach the next corner, mark ¹/₄" from edge of table runner top.

Fig. 4   Fig. 5

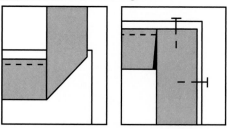

9. Backstitching at edge of table runner, sew pinned binding to table runner (Fig. 6), backstitching when you reach the next mark. Lift needle out of fabric and clip thread.

Fig. 6

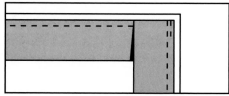

10. Repeat Steps 8 and 9 to continue sewing binding to table runner until binding overlaps beginning end by 2". Trim excess binding.

11. On one edge of table runner, fold binding over to backing and pin pressed edge in place, covering stitching line (Fig. 7). On adjacent side, fold binding over, forming a mitered corner (Fig. 8). Repeat to pin remainder of binding in place.

Fig. 7   Fig. 8

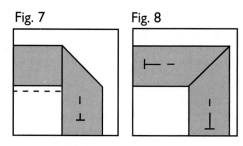

12. Blindstitch binding to backing, taking care not to stitch through to front of table runner.

FRAMED SAMPLER
(page 14)

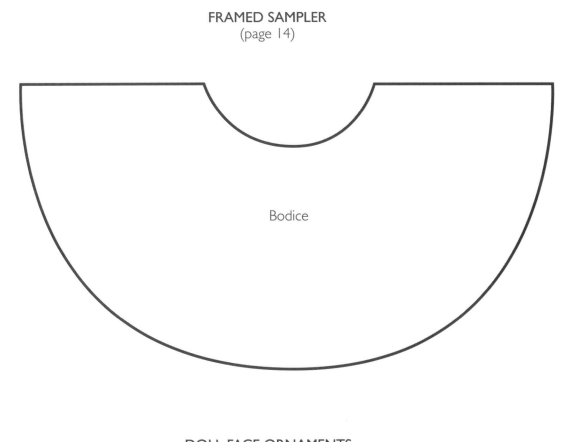

Bodice

DOLL FACE ORNAMENTS
(page 12)

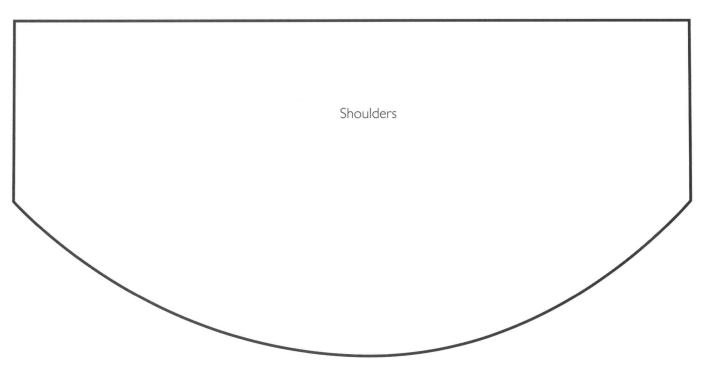

Shoulders

A Rag Doll
she may be,
But she always
has a
hug for me

FRAMED SAMPLER
(page 14)

MINI SAMPLERS
(page 13)

RAG DOLL
(page 13)

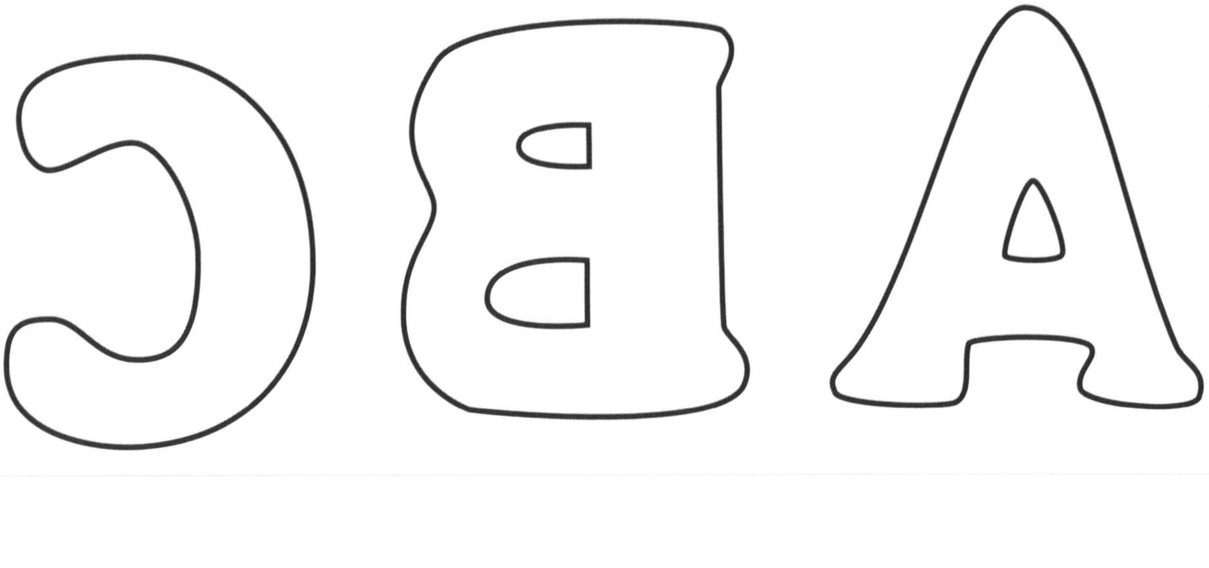

A B C

142

CARROT ICICLES
(page 37)

Carrot

SODA-BOTTLE SNOWMEN
(page 38)

Hat Brim

SNOW SCENE
ORNAMENTS
(page 37)

Mitten

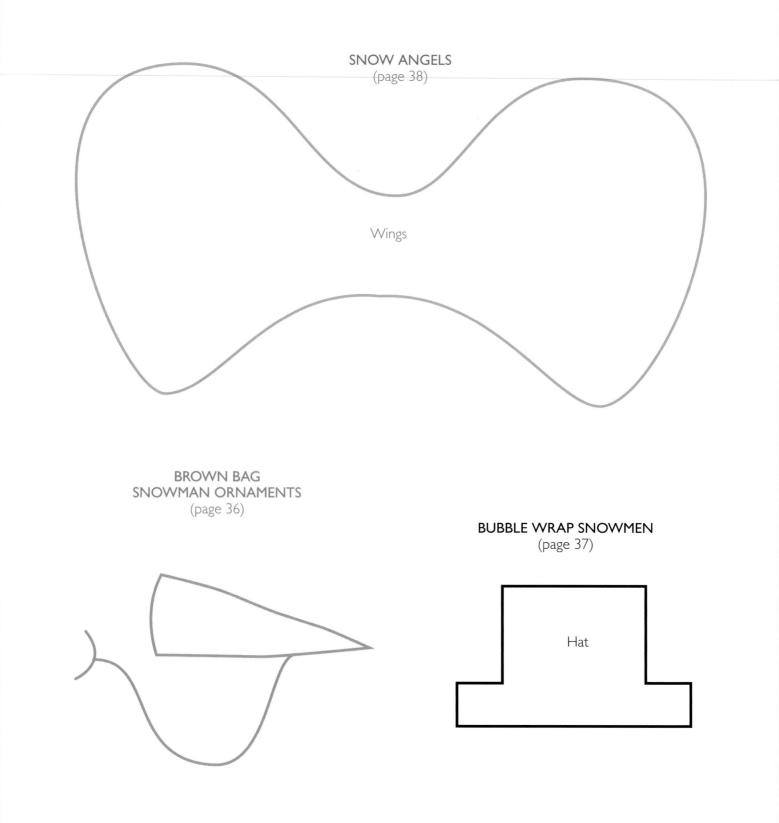

SNOW ANGELS
(page 38)

Wings

BROWN BAG
SNOWMAN ORNAMENTS
(page 36)

BUBBLE WRAP SNOWMEN
(page 37)

Hat

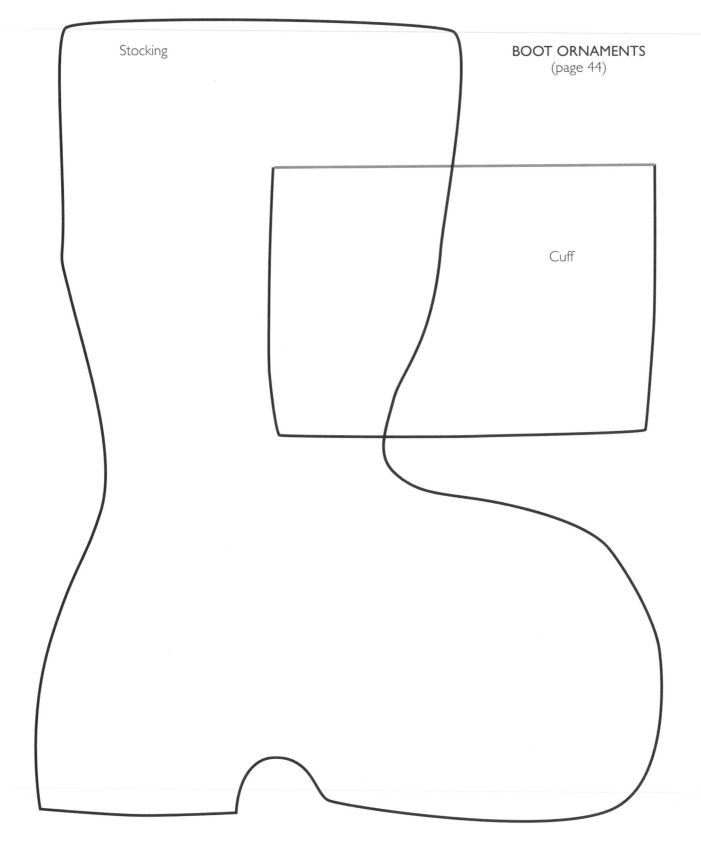

Stocking

BOOT ORNAMENTS
(page 44)

Cuff

STUFFED SANTA
(page 55)

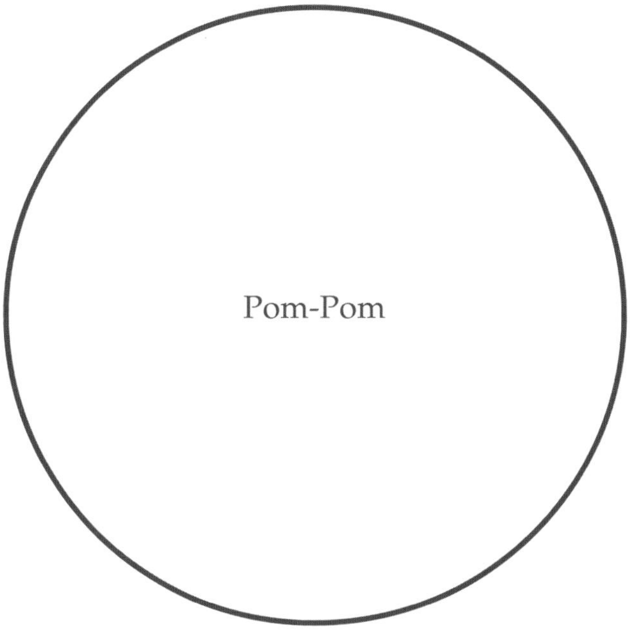

Pom-Pom

WINTRY WALL HANGING
(page 88)

Let it snow

LADIES' TWIN SET
(page 89)

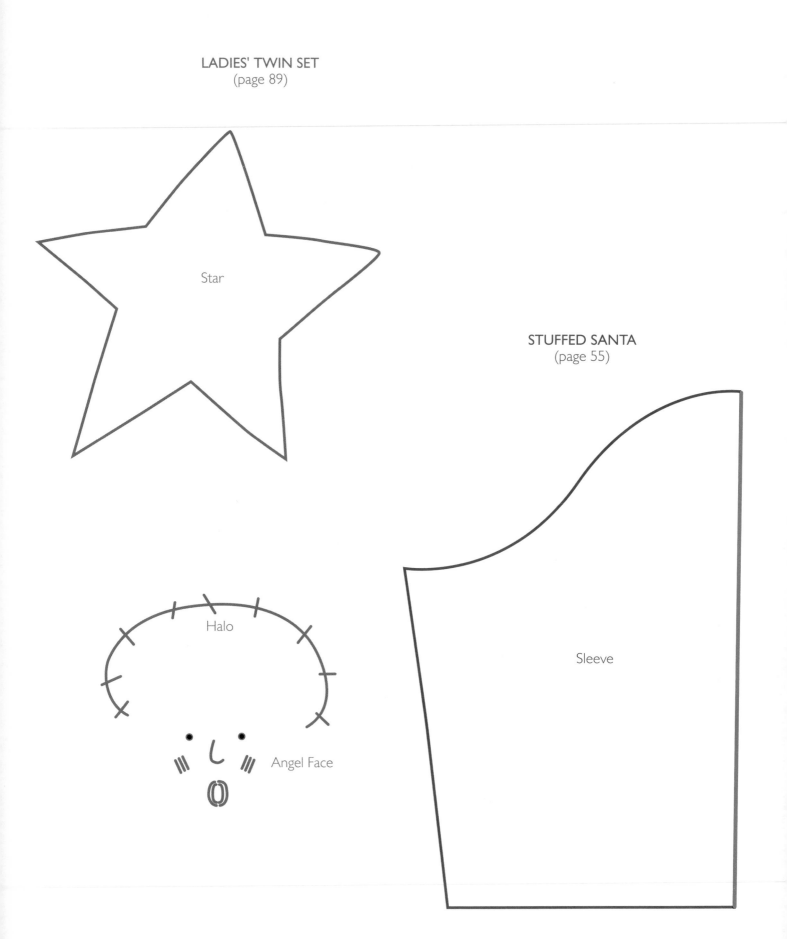

Star

STUFFED SANTA
(page 55)

Halo

Angel Face

Sleeve

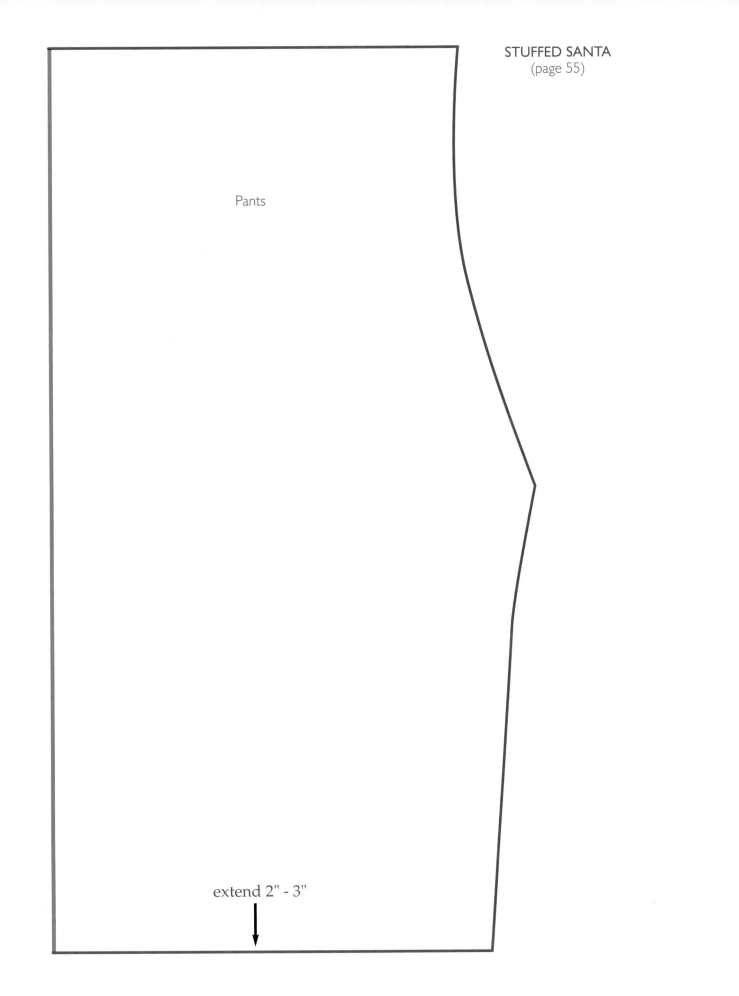

STUFFED SANTA
(page 55)

Pants

extend 2" - 3"

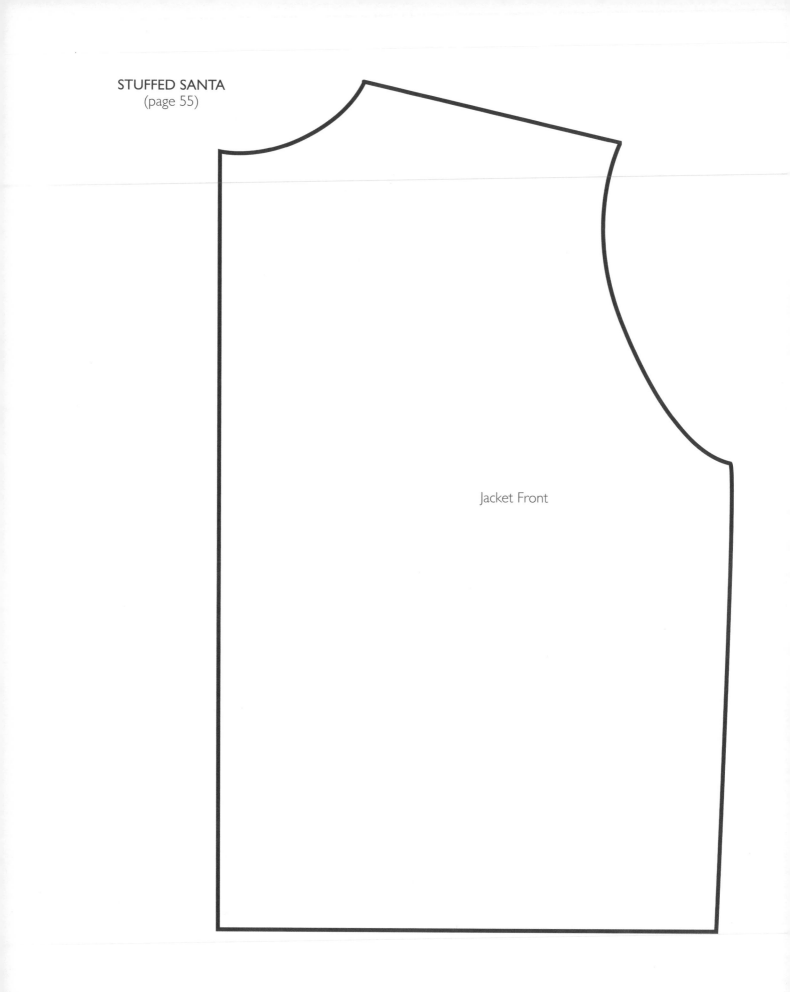

Jacket Front

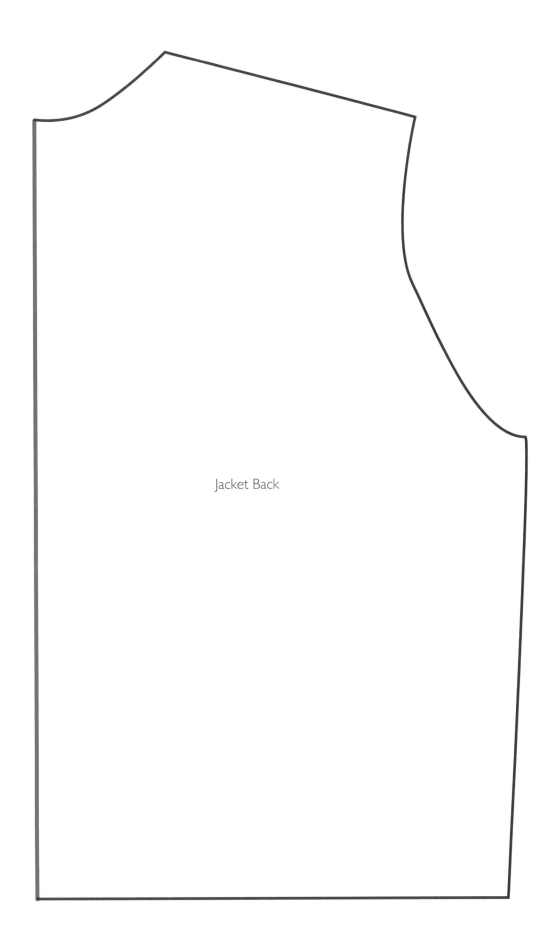

Jacket Back

Trunk

Palm Frond

Palm Frond

153

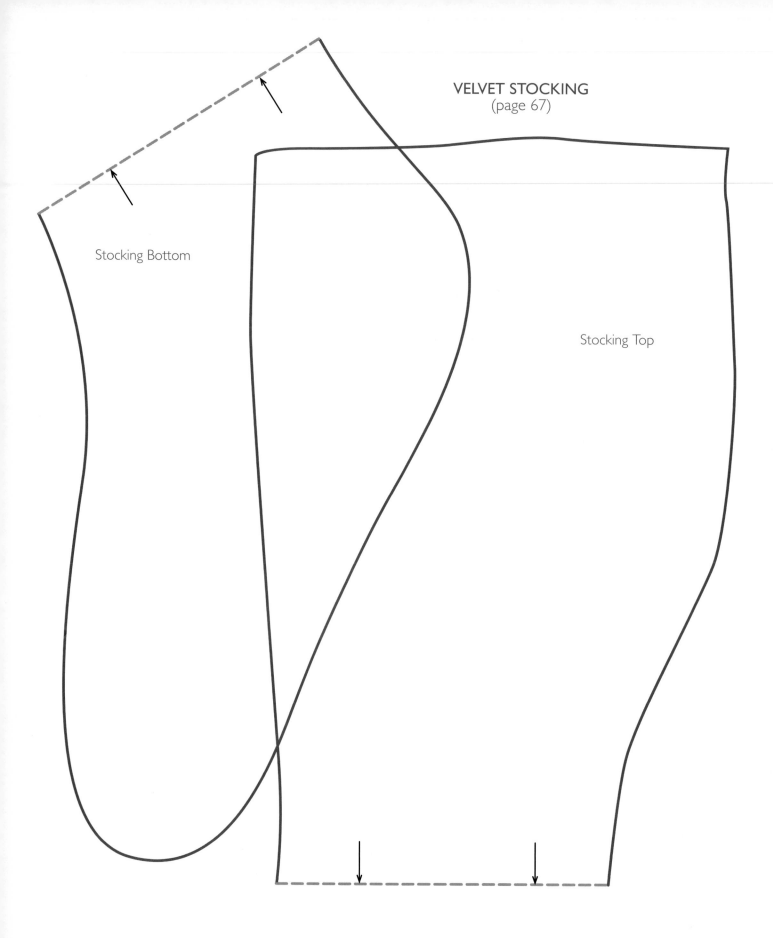

VELVET STOCKING
(page 67)

Stocking Bottom

Stocking Top

NOEL BAG
(page 135)

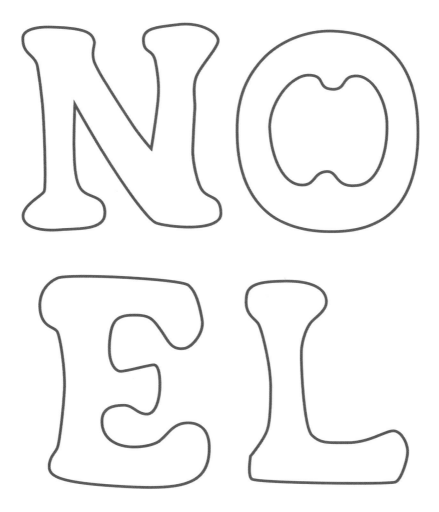

PATCHWORK MEMORY ALBUM
(page 88)

GENERAL INSTRUCTIONS

MAKING PATTERNS

When entire pattern is shown, place tracing paper over pattern and trace pattern. For a more durable pattern, use a permanent marker to trace pattern onto stencil plastic.

When pattern pieces are stacked or overlapped, place tracing paper over pattern and follow a single color to trace pattern. Repeat to trace each pattern separately onto tracing paper.

When only half of pattern is shown (indicated by blue line on pattern), fold tracing paper in half and match fold of paper to blue line of pattern. Trace pattern half; turn folded paper over and draw over traced lines on remaining side of paper.

SEWING SHAPES

1. Center pattern on wrong side of one fabric piece and use fabric marking pen to draw around pattern. Do not cut out shape.
2. Place fabric pieces right sides together. Leaving an opening for turning, carefully sew pieces together directly on drawn line.
3. Leaving a 1/4" seam allowance, cut out shape. Clip seam allowance at curves and corners. Turn right side out and press.

MAKING APPLIQUÉS

To prevent darker fabrics from showing through, white or light-colored fabrics may need to be lined with fusible interfacing before applying paper-backed fusible web.

To make reverse appliqué pieces, trace pattern onto tracing paper; turn traced paper over and continue to follow all steps using reversed pattern.

1. Use a pencil to trace pattern or draw around reversed pattern onto paper side of web as many times as indicated for a single fabric. Repeat for additional patterns and fabrics.
2. Follow manufacturer's instructions to fuse traced patterns to wrong side of fabrics. Do not remove paper backing.
3. Cut out appliqué pieces along traced lines. Remove paper backing.
4. Arrange appliqués, web side down, on project, overlapping as necessary. Appliqués can be temporarily held in place by touching appliqués with tip of iron. If appliqués are not in desired position, lift and reposition.
5. Fuse appliqués in place.

MACHINE APPLIQUÉ

1. Place paper or stabilizer on wrong side of background fabric under fused appliqué.
2. Beginning on a straight edge of appliqué if possible, position project under presser foot so that most of stitching will be on appliqué. Take a stitch in fabric and bring bobbin thread to top. Hold both threads toward you and sew over them for several stitches to secure; clip threads. Using a medium-width zigzag stitch, stitch over all exposed raw edges of appliqué(s) and along detail lines as indicated in instructions.
3. When stitching is complete, remove stabilizer. Clip threads close to stitching.

CUTTING A FABRIC CIRCLE

1. Cut a square of fabric the size indicated in project instructions.
2. Matching right sides, fold fabric square in half from top to bottom and again from left to right.
3. Tie one end of string to a pencil or fabric marking pen. Measuring from pencil, insert a thumbtack through string at length indicated in project instructions. Insert thumbtack through folded corner of fabric. Holding tack in place and keeping string taut, mark cutting line (Fig. 1).

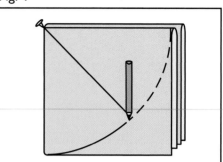

Fig. 1

4. Cut along drawn line through all fabric layers.

COVERING A LAMPSHADE

1. To make pattern, find seamline of lampshade. If shade does not have a seamline, draw a vertical line from top of shade to bottom edge of shade.
2. Center tissue paper edge on shade seamline; tape in place. Wrap paper around shade extending one inch past seamline; tape to secure (Fig. 1).

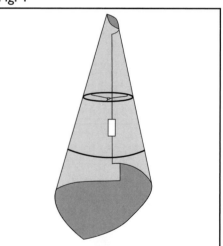

Fig. 1

3. Trace along top and bottom edges of shade. Draw vertical line from top edge to bottom edge of shade 1" past seamline. Remove paper; cut along drawn lines.
4. Use pattern to cut cover from desired fabric.
5. Fold one straight edge of covering 1/2" to wrong side; press.
6. Matching unpressed straight edge of covering to seamline, use spray adhesive to apply covering to shade. Use glue to secure pressed edge.

MAKING A BOW

Note: Loop sizes given in project instructions refer to the length of ribbon used to make one loop of bow.

1. For first streamer, measure desired length of streamer from one end of ribbon; twist ribbon between fingers (Fig. 1).

Fig. 1

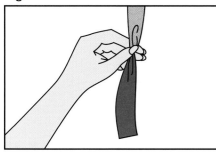

2. Keeping right side of ribbon facing out, fold ribbon to front to form desired-size loop; gather ribbon between fingers (Fig. 2). Fold ribbon to back to form another loop; gather ribbon between fingers (Fig. 3).

Fig. 2

Fig. 3

3. (*Note:* If a center loop is desired, form half the desired number of loops, then loosely wrap ribbon around thumb and gather ribbon between fingers as shown in Fig. 4;

form remaining loops.) Continue to form loops, varying size of loops as desired, until bow is desired size.

Fig. 4

4. For remaining streamer, trim ribbon to desired length.
5. To secure bow, hold gathered loops tightly. Fold a length of floral wire around gathers of loops. Hold wire ends behind bow, gathering all loops forward; twist bow to tighten wire. Arrange loops and trim ribbon ends as desired.

MAKING A POM-POM

Multiply finished pom-pom size (stated in project instructions) by 2. Cut a square of cardboard the determined measurement. (*Note:* The more yarn used the fuller the pom-pom will be.) Wind yarn around cardboard the desired number of times (if using more than one color yarn, wrap yarns at the same time); clip ends of yarn even with cardboard. Carefully slip yarn off the cardboard and firmly knot an 18" length of yarn around center. Leave yarn ends long enough to attach pom-pom to project or cut even with lengths in pom-pom. Cut loops and trim to shape pom-pom into a smooth ball. Fluff pom-pom by rolling between hands.

PAINTING TECHNIQUES
PREPARING PROJECT

If painting on a garment, wash, dry, and press garment according to paint manufacturer's recommendations. Insert T-shirt form or iron shiny side of freezer paper to wrong side of garment under area to be painted.

TRANSFERRING PATTERNS

Trace pattern onto tracing paper. Using removable tape, tape pattern to project. Place transfer paper coated side down between project and tracing paper (using old transfer paper will help prevent smudges). If transferring pattern onto a dark surface, use light-colored transfer paper to transfer pattern. Use a pencil to transfer outlines of base coat areas of design to project (press lightly to avoid smudges and heavy lines that are difficult to cover). If necessary, use a soft eraser to remove any smudges.

PAINTING BASE COATS

(*Note:* A disposable plate makes a good palette.) Use medium round brush for large areas and a small round brush for small areas. Do not overload brush. Let paint dry between coats.

TRANSFERRING DETAILS

To transfer detail lines to design, replace pattern and transfer paper over painted base coats and use stylus to lightly transfer detail lines onto project.

PAINTING DETAILS

Side loading (shading and highlighting): Dip one corner of a flat brush in water; blot on a paper towel. Dip dry corner of brush into paint. Stroke brush back and forth on palette until there is a gradual change from paint to water in each brush stroke. Stroke loaded side of brush along detail line on project, pulling brush toward you and turning project if necessary. For shading, side load brush with a darker color of paint. For highlighting, side load brush with lighter color of paint.
Line work: Let paint dry before beginning line work to prevent smudging lines or ruining pen. Draw over detail lines with permanent pen.
Dots: Dip the tip of a round paintbrush, the handle end of a paintbrush, or one end of a toothpick in paint and touch to project. Dip in paint each time for uniform dots.

GENERAL INSTRUCTIONS (continued)

Sponge painting: Lightly dampen sponge piece. Dip sponge piece into paint and blot on paper towel to remove excess paint. Use a stamping motion to apply paint. Reapply paint to sponge as necessary.

Spatter painting: Dip bristle tips of toothbrush into paint, blot on paper towel to remove excess. Pull thumb across bristles to spatter paint over desired area. Repeat to achieve desired effect.

TIPS FOR PAINTING ON FABRIC

To help stabilize a fabric item, iron freezer paper (coated side down toward fabric) on wrong side of area to be painted. Remove freezer paper when painting is complete.

EMBROIDERY STITCHES
BACKSTITCH

Bring needle up at 1; go down at 2. Bring needle up at 3 and back down at 1 (Fig. 1). Continue working to make a continuous line of stitches.

Fig. 1

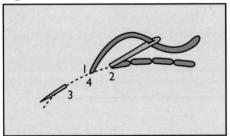

BLANKET STITCH

Bring needle up at 1; keeping thread below point of needle, go down at 2 and up at 3 (Fig. 2). Continue working as shown in Fig. 3.

Fig. 2

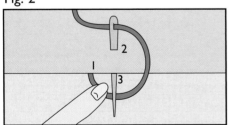

Fig. 3

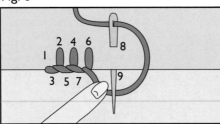

CROSS STITCH

Bring needle up at 1 and go down at 2. Come up at 3 and go down at 4 (Fig. 4).

Fig. 4

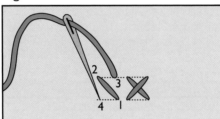

FRENCH KNOT

Bring needle up at 1. Wrap thread once around needle and insert needle at 2, holding thread with non-stitching fingers (Fig. 5). Tighten knot as close to fabric as possible while pulling needle back through fabric.

Fig. 5

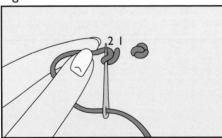

OVERCAST STITCH

Bring needle up at 1; take thread over edge of fabric and bring needle up at 2. Continue stitching along edge of fabric (Fig. 6).

Fig. 6

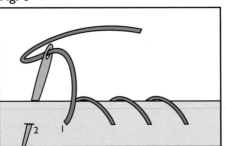

RUNNING STITCH

Make a series of straight stitches with stitch length equal to the space between stitches (Fig. 7).

Fig. 7

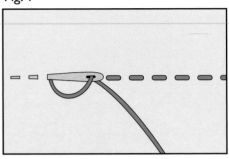

STRAIGHT STITCH

Bring needle up at 1 and take needle down at 2 (Fig. 8). Length of stitches may be varied as desired.

Fig. 8

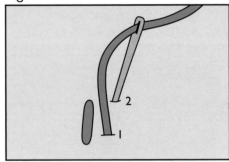

CROSS STITCH
COUNTED CROSS STITCH (X):

Work one Cross Stitch for each colored square on chart. For horizontal rows, work stitches in two journeys (Fig. 1). For vertical rows, complete each stitch as shown in Fig. 2. When the chart shows a Backstitch crossing a colored square (Fig. 3), work the Cross Stitch first, then work the Backstitch over the Cross Stitch.

Fig. 1

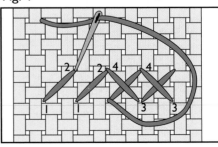

Fig. 2

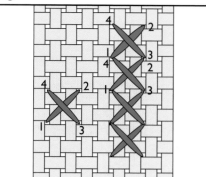

Fig. 3

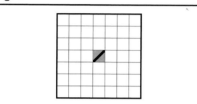

QUARTER STITCH (¹/₄X):

Quarter Stitches are shown as triangular shapes of color in chart and color key. Come up at 1 (Fig. 4), then split fabric thread to take needle down at 2.

Fig. 4

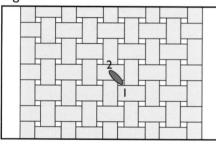

BACKSTITCH (B'ST):

For outline or details, Backstitch (shown in chart and color key by colored straight lines) should be worked after the design has been completed (Fig. 5).

Fig. 5

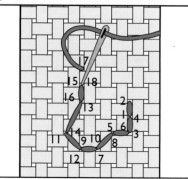

CROCHET

ABBREVIATIONS

ch(s)	chain(s)
dc	double crochet(s)
hdc	half double crochet(s)
mm	millimeters
Rnd(s)	Round(s)
sc	single crochet(s)
sp(s)	space(s)
st(s)	stitch(es)
YO	yarn over

★ - work instructions following ★ as many **more** times as indicated in addition to the first time.

† to † - work all instructions from first † to second † **as many** times as specified.

( ) or [ ] - work enclosed instructions **as many** times as specified by the number immediately following **or** work all enclosed instructions in the stitch or space indicated **or** contains explanatory remarks.

colon (:) - the number(s) given after a colon at the end of a row or round denote(s) the number of stitches you should have on that row or round.

SLIP STITCH (slip st): To work a slip stitch, insert hook in stitch indicated, YO and draw yarn through stitch and loop on hook (Fig. 1). To join with a slip stitch, begin with a slip knot on hook, insert hook in stitch indicated, YO and draw yarn through stitch and through the slip knot on hook.

Fig. 1

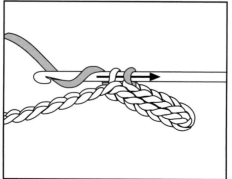

SINGLE CROCHET (sc): To work a single crochet, insert hook in stitch or space indicated, YO and pull up a loop, YO and draw yarn through both loops on hook (Fig. 2).

Fig. 2

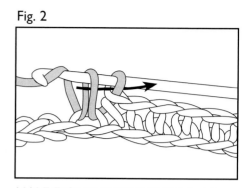

HALF DOUBLE CROCHET (hdc): To work a half double crochet, YO, insert hook in stitch or space indicated, YO and pull up a loop (3 loops on hook), YO and draw yarn through all 3 loops on hook (Fig. 3).

Fig. 3

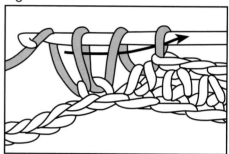

DOUBLE CROCHET (dc): To work a double crochet, YO, insert hook in stitch or space indicated, YO and pull up a loop (3 loops on hook), YO and draw yarn through 2 loops on hook (Fig. 4) (2 loops remain on hook), YO and draw yarn through remaining 2 loops on hook (Fig. 5).

Fig. 4

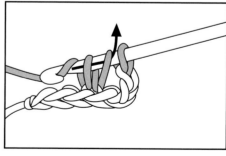

Fig. 5

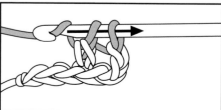

CREDITS

We want to extend a warm *thank you* to the generous people who allowed us to photograph our projects at their homes.

- *"C" Is for Christmas:* Paul and Becky Owen
- *Journey to Bethlehem:* Shirley Held
- *Tartan Classics:* Ben and Brenda Hogan
- *You Can Build a Snowman!:* Ellison Poe
- *Sportsman's Holiday:* Dean and Lori Downs
- *Santa's Workshop:* Wes and Sue Ann Hall
- *A "Bead-Dazzled" Christmas:* Robert Ginnaven
- *Terrific Tablescapes:* Chuck and Nancy Banks, Shirley Held, and Charles and Peg Mills

A special thanks goes to the following business for permitting us to photograph projects on their premises.

- *Terrific Tablescapes:* The Empress of Little Rock Bed and Breakfast, 2120 Louisiana Street, Little Rock, Arkansas 72206

We would like to recognize Dan River Inc., of New York, New York, for fabrics used in *"C" Is for Christmas* and *Tartan Classics.*

A special thanks is also extended to Frankie Roberts for the use of Christmas dishes in *Terrific Tablescapes.*

To Magna IV Color Imaging of Little Rock, Arkansas, we say thank you for the superb color reproduction and excellent pre-press preparation.

Our sincere appreciation goes to photographers Ken West, Larry Pennington, and Mark Mathews of Peerless Photography, Little Rock, Arkansas; and Jerry R. Davis of Jerry Davis Photography, Little Rock, Arkansas, for their excellent photography.

To the talented people who helped in the creation of the following projects and recipes in this book, we extend a special word of thanks.

- *Stitched Clock Ornaments,* page 23: Holly DeFount of Kooler Design Studio, Inc.
- *Cozy Crocheted Afghan,* page 79: Terry Kimbrough
- *Patchwork Memory Album, Wintry Wall Hanging,* and *Flannel Gift Bags,* pages 80-81: Holly Witt for Banar Designs
- *Beaded Jewelry,* pages 84-85: Guniz Jernigan
- *Pumpkin Pie Cake,* page 107: Willia Mae Honold
- *Christmas Stockings,* page 111, and *Golden Lemon Stars,* page 130: Becky Werle
- *Lobster Bisque,* page 123: Lucille A. Pulliam
- *Homer's Award-Winning Fruitcake,* page 127: Homer Rogers

We are sincerely grateful to the people who assisted in making and testing the projects in this book: Ruth Epperson and Ruby J. Solida.